BEER HIKING

SOUTHERN CALIFORNIA

THE TASTIEST WAY TO DISCOVER SoCAL'S BEACHES, MOUNTAINS, AND DESERTS

Beer Hiking Southern California
The Tastiest Way to Discover SoCal's Beaches, Mountains, and Deserts

By: Johanna Flashman

ISBN: 978-3-03964-034-8
Published by Helvetiq, Lausanne/Basel, Switzerland
Graphic Design and illustration: Daniel Malak, Jędrzej Malak (maps)
Printed in China
First Edition April 2024

www.helvetiq.com/us
www.facebook.com/helvetiq_usa
instagram: @helvetiq_usa

helvetiq.com

MIX
Paper from
responsible sources
FSC® C167893

BEER HIKING SOUTHERN CALIFORNIA

THE TASTIEST WAY TO DISCOVER SoCAL'S BEACHES, MOUNTAINS, AND DESERTS

TABLE OF CONTENTS

1

INTRODUCTION

ABOUT THE AUTHOR

Johanna Flashman is an avid outdoorswoman, outdoor and travel writer, and beer drinker. Growing up in Oakland, California, she had towering redwoods, foggy beaches, and mountainous vistas at her fingertips and fell in love with the natural environment. After several years in Europe—university in Scotland, trail running in the French Alps, bike touring in Iceland—she returned to the Golden State in 2022 to explore the beaches, mountains, and deserts of Southern California for this book. She started off at ground level in her cousin's Sprinter van and midway through decided to fully commit to the van life with her own ProMaster.

Johanna had her first taste of beer at the age of two when her parents gave her a sip—and she reached for more. After a legally appropriate nineteen-year gap, she returned to beer but this time with a more refined palate and an interest in craft brewing. Starting with the malty sweetness of stouts and expanding to sours and eventually more typical blondes, lagers, and IPAs, she has loved exploring new tastes and styles of beer.

Johanna got into writing as a way to tell people's stories, help others learn about and appreciate the natural environment, and make the outdoors more accessible. Her writing has appeared in print and online publications including *Outside*, *Climbing*, *National Geographic Travel*, and *SELF*. She has created her own platform, *The Freelance Outdoorswoman,* to showcase women freelancers in the outdoor industry. Writing this book has been the perfect combination of her passions—she's had the opportunity to nerd out about plant and animal ecology and get to know folks making a difference in the world one beer at a time.

You can follow Johanna's ongoing van life and travel adventures on Instagram @jo_flashman and at johannaflashman.com.

ABOUT BEER HIKING IN SOUTHERN CALIFORNIA

While Southern California may be best known for its warm beaches and wealthy celebrities, it is also a hiker's paradise with thousands of miles of well-maintained trails. From urban escapes to rural wilderness, Southern California has it all. And for those who like a postadventure brew, the region is an absolute gold mine. The state as a whole has over 1,100 breweries—more than any other state in the country. In Southern California alone, there are over 450.

SoCal is one of the most diverse regions in the country both culturally and ecologically, with bustling cities like Los Angeles and San Diego along with snow-capped mountains, stunning ocean beaches, and wild deserts. With forested canyons, sparkling waterfalls, high mountain peaks, coastal headlands, high-altitude deserts, and isolated islands, Southern California has a hike for every taste and ability. And once you've finished walking, you can almost always find a welcoming spot serving up fresh craft beer to drink with friends as you bask in the triumph of another successful hike.

The precise classification of what constitutes Southern California is up for debate and depends on whom you ask. For the purposes of this book, Southern California comprises 56,505 square miles and ten counties, from Kern and San Luis Obispo Counties in the north down to the border with Mexico. The easternmost hike in this book is in Joshua Tree National Park; while further east there are some exceptional hikes, like those in Mojave National Preserve, they are far more isolated and lack a nearby brewery. For a similar reason, there are no hikes included in Imperial County, which has some worthwhile breweries but lacks any hikes within a 20-mile radius of them.

The featured hikes are primarily concentrated near the largest metropolitan areas in Los Angeles County and San Diego County, but you'll find hikes in this book in every county aside from Imperial. Whale watching on your way to the Channel Islands, exploring a narrow slot canyon in Solana Beach, or summiting the iconic Mount Baldy, you'll find each hike has its own charm. From little-known local favorites to SoCal classics, these hikes lead through dense chaparral and coastal sage scrub biomes, towering pine forests and wide-open fields of wildflowers.

Similarly, each brewery and beer you'll come across has its own special flair. While you'll find the regional favorite West Coast IPA widely available, almost every brewery offers a diverse lineup of brews to suit every preference. Along with beer quality, one of the highlights of Southern California breweries is the community they offer. Even in a region with over 23 million residents, when you walk into many of these small, family-owned breweries, you become family yourself.

From tourists looking to explore beyond Disneyland and Hollywood to outdoorsy locals wanting to add variety to their regular favorites, anyone who loves hiking and beer will find inspiration in the pages of this book. Good times and new adventures await you. Have fun, hike safely, and drink responsibly.

LAND ACKNOWLEDGEMENT

It would be a disservice not to acknowledge that every hiking region within these pages was originally and continues to be inhabited and cared for by Native peoples. Thirteen different original tribal territories make up the area covered in this book. Today, these territories are home to over thirty different federally recognized tribes.

Throughout the pages of this book, you'll find facts about plants Native peoples used, cultural history about former and current tribal communities and organizations, and other relevant information. If any of these catch your curiosity, consider visiting one of the museums in Southern California dedicated to Native history and culture or donating to Native-led nonprofits to support their ongoing work.

These are a few suggestions, but there are many others as well:

Museums:
www.chumashmuseum.org
www.baronamuseum.com
www.malkimuseum.org
www.parks.ca.gov/?page_id=24096
www.visionaguacaliente.com
www.shermanindian.org/museum
www.nuuicunni.com
www.savesouthwestmuseum.com

Organizations:
www.firstnations.org
www.scairinc.org
http://indiancenter.org/

CHOOSE THE BEER OR THE HIKE

HIKE LOCATION ——————→

REGION ——————

MAP ——————→

WEIR CANYON
MARVEL AT SPRING WILDFLOWER BLOOMS

ANAHEIM

▷⋯ STARTING POINT	✕ DESTINATION
S. HIDDEN CANYON RD.	POPPY FIELDS
🍺 BREWERY	HIKE TYPE
GREEN CHEEK BEER COMPANY	EASY
🐾 DOG FRIENDLY	SEASON
YES (LEASH REQUIRED)	FEBRUARY–APRIL
$ FEES	⏱ DURATION
NONE	1 HOUR 30 MIN.
⚠ MAP REFERENCE	↦ LENGTH
SANTIAGO OAKS REGIONAL PARK (POSTED AT TRAILHEAD)	3.8 MILES (LOLLIPOP LOOP)
⊙ HIGHLIGHTS	∿ ELEVATION GAIN
WILDFLOWERS	640 FEET

218

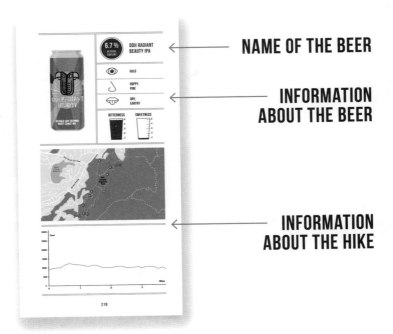

6.7% ALCOHOL CONTENT — DDH RADIANT BEAUTY IPA

GOLD

HOPPY, PINE

DRY, EARTHY

BITTERNESS   SWEETNESS

219

←—————— **NAME OF THE BEER**

←—————— **INFORMATION ABOUT THE BEER**

←—————— **INFORMATION ABOUT THE HIKE**

ON THE HIKES AND HIKE RATINGS

The hikes in this guide range from easy urban strolls to full-day mountain summits. Each route is given a subjective difficulty rating of easy, moderate, or strenuous. These ratings are based on my personal experience along with trail factors including length, elevation gain, trail conditions, and online reviews. Your experience with the hikes may differ from these ratings; some moderate hikes might feel easier or more strenuous to you than they did to me.

EASY

All but one of the easy hikes are less than 4 miles long. They generally have an elevation gain of 500 feet or less. Many of them are on wide, well-maintained routes and two are wheelchair-friendly.

MODERATE

The majority of the trails in this guide are classified as moderate. Be sure to check the specific mileage, elevation gain, and description. Some are shorter—less than 4 miles—but have a greater elevation gain. Some toe the line between moderate and strenuous and, depending on the day, might lean more towards strenuous. Most are on well-marked trails, but some require a little route finding or careful foot placement, while others involve getting your feet wet during river crossings. All have less than 2,000 feet of elevation gain.

STRENUOUS

The hardest hikes in the book, these trails are especially long or steep, or a combination of both. Many climb to a mountain peak. Some require scrambling or a fair amount of route finding. All of them will have at least some feature that would be less than ideal for a beginning hiker. This rating has the widest mileage range, from just 2.7 miles (with several sections of scrambling) to almost 12 miles.

While each hike has a specific rating, the beauty of the book being in *your* hands is that you can make use of it as you wish. Don't feel obligated to hike the exact route described in the book. Instead, think of the proposed hikes as suggestions that you can alter to fit your ability. Many of the easier hikes can be extended and made more difficult; conversely, many of the strenuous hikes can be shortened and still offer worthwhile outings—especially if you aren't attached to summiting.

The author completed all the hikes over a 9-month period (winter, spring, and summer). During this time, California had record amounts of rain, which led to abundant rivers and waterfalls and a phenomenal superbloom. There were also landslides that decimated trail infrastructure and record-breaking heat waves that made hiking impossible for a time. Some trails have not been featured because they've been closed for over two years due to excessive wildfire damage. With climate change, extreme weather events will likely persist and even get worse; what is a pristine old-growth forest today might be the remnants of a wildfire tomorrow. While this is a sobering fact, it's important to remember so we can appreciate and care for these precious lands. Always check with land managers to confirm a trail's status before you set out. Know that trails change over time and may not exactly fit the turn-by-turn directions presented in this book.

A number of hikes require a fee of some sort (i.e., entrance, parking, transportation, etc.). A few of these fees are included in the state parks California Explorer Pass or the national parks America the Beautiful Pass, meaning that entrance is free if you have the corresponding pass. This is noted in the hike infographic where it is the case. You can purchase passes in person at many of the participating parks or online at the California State Parks store (state passes) or USGS store (national passes).

Over three-quarters of the hikes allow dogs, but most require leashes; please respect these regulations for the safety of both your dog and the local environment.

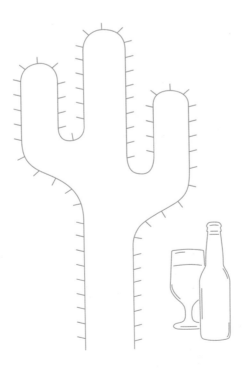

ON THE BREWERIES AND BEER RATINGS

The featured beers for each chapter were chosen because they are customer favorites or flagship brews, have a special history, or were simply what the author felt fit the weather and hike at the time of her visit. Many are flagships available year-round, but some breweries rotate their beer offerings regularly and some brews are strictly seasonal. Rest assured, each brewery has many more delightful beers available than the featured one, and most offer taster flights so you can explore your options before committing to a full pint.

With so many breweries throughout Southern California, there were far more options than could be included in this book. In many cases, for each featured brewery, there were three other equally good establishments that didn't make it in. A few select spots that regrettably aren't in the book but are well worth a visit include Liquid Gravity, Euryale Brewing, California Wild Ales, Nickel Brewing, 3 Punk Ales, Border X Brewing, Hillcrest Brewing, Syncopated Brewing, and Smoking Cannon Brewery.

As I chose the breweries, I considered online ratings, beer quality, atmosphere, friendliness, and food offerings but also ownership, and prioritized breweries owned and operated by minorities or women. There are far fewer of these breweries, and I wanted to highlight the different experiences these breweries offer and demonstrate to future brewers and beer lovers that brewing and enjoying beer should be for everyone (of legal age). There are also many breweries in the book with women and people of color in co-ownership or leadership positions as part of a husband-and-wife or brother-and-sister team or a group of friends. I have noted women- and minority-owned breweries in the highlights section of the infographics, while co-ownership structures are discussed in the brewery descriptions.

There are also several great breweries in SoCal that are openly queer owned. Unfortunately, either I couldn't match these with the featured hikes, or else they were located too near other breweries that were unmissable. I look forward to featuring queer-owned breweries in a future update to this book.

The majority of the trailheads and breweries in this book require a vehicle to reach. Drink responsibly and never drink and drive. Have a designated driver or wait at least 45 minutes per beer for the alcohol to clear your system before getting behind the wheel. Alternatively, pick up a growler, six-pack, or can to-go and enjoy responsibly back at your home, campsite, RV, or hotel.

PREPARING FOR YOUR HIKE

THE TEN ESSENTIALS

The ten essentials are the gold standard of baseline preparedness in the outdoors. Know them. Bring them. If you're unsure if you need a given item, err on the side of preparedness and bring it—you'll be glad you have it in an emergency. As a general rule, the longer, more rugged, and less populated trails require more gear and preparation.

- **Navigation.** The maps in this book are for reference only. The most reliable tools for navigation are a print map in a Ziploc bag, a compass, and the knowledge of how to use them. These days, a phone with a downloaded map can go a long way, but a phone can break or run out of battery, so you don't want it to be your only option.
- **Hydration.** Especially in the Southern California heat, bringing enough water is essential. Bring more than you think you'll need.
- **Nutrition.** Part of the fun of hiking is eating food in beautiful places, so bring plenty of high-energy snacks and lunch foods for the time you expect to be out—and then some.
- **Sun Protection.** Sunburn is no joke in sunny Southern California. Apply sunscreen generously and wear a brimmed hat and sunglasses. For even more protection, consider sun-protective clothing like a sun hoodie and long, breathable pants.
- **Insulation.** Weather can change quickly. Tuck in an extra "just in case" layer on top of the layers you plan to wear. This could be a windbreaker, puffy, rain jacket, or something else, depending on conditions.
- **Illumination.** Sometimes hikes take longer than you expect. If you get caught after dark, having a light source is essential. A flashlight is good. A headlamp (with extra batteries) is better.
- **Fire.** In an emergency, fire can be used as a signal or source of heat. Many areas of Southern California have fire restrictions, especially during fire season, so be aware of the restrictions in your area.
- **First aid.** From minor cuts and blisters to more serious injuries, you need to be prepared. A small first-aid kit and the knowledge of how to use everything in it can go a long way to keeping you safe and comfortable on the trail.
- **Tools.** A pocketknife or multi-tool can take on big jobs on the trail. A small whistle can help alert rescuers if needed (you may find one attached to your hiking pack). And never underestimate duct tape—you can wrap some around your water bottle as a convenient way to carry it!
- **Shelter.** In an emergency overnight, some form of shelter to protect you from the elements can be lifesaving. Something as simple as a space blanket or small tarp can make a big difference.

HIKING SEASON

The hiking season is listed for each individual hike. With Southern California's diverse range of ecosystems, there's no one specific season, though much of the region is too hot for comfortable hiking from July through September and the mountains may be too snowy in the winter. Heat-related illnesses in the summer are no joke. This also goes for your dog—if it's above 80°F, it's likely too hot to hike with your dog!

HUNTING SEASONS

Hunting seasons and rules in California vary depending on the location, animal, and weapon. Most hunting happens in the autumn. Many areas restrict hunting near hiking trails, so the best practice is to stay on the trail and have some pieces of safety orange available to wear if needed. For more information about hunting seasons and regulations in California, visit the California Department of Fish and Wildlife, www.wildlife.ca.gov/Hunting.

WEATHER

Southern California is known for its hot, sunny weather, but it can get cold in some areas! The mountains east of Los Angeles get snow in the winter and can have unpredictable alpine weather, while the desert and inland areas regularly break triple digits in the summer. For accurate forecasts, check the National Weather Service at www.weather.gov.

WILDLIFE SAFETY

Southern California may not have the same level of wildlife danger as some parts of the world, but it is home to several animals that can be dangerous to hikers—namely, rattlesnakes, bears, and mountain lions (oh my!). None of these are innately aggressive or out to cause harm to humans, but they can and will if threatened. Watch where you're stepping and listen for the telltale rattle of a snake—don't wear noise-canceling headphones or you may not hear the snake's warning! Make noise along the trail to ensure you don't surprise bears and mountain lions and so they can steer clear of you. Do not feed or approach any wildlife.

ADDITIONAL RESOURCES

For much more information on additional hikes and breweries and further visitor guides describing dining, lodging, camping, and other attractions, check out these sites:

KERN

Hiking: AllTrails,
www.alltrails.com

Breweries: Bakersfield Brewery Trail,
www.visitbakersfield.com/restaurants/brewery-trail/

Visitor Amenities: Kern River Valley Chamber of Commerce,
www.kernrivervalley.com/

SAN LUIS OBISPO

Hiking: Hiking & Trails in SLO CAL,
www.slocal.com/things-to-do/outdoor-activities/hiking-trails/

Breweries: Central Coast Brewers Guild,
www.centralcoastbrewersguild.com/

Visitor Amenities: Visit SLO CAL,
www.slocal.com/

SANTA BARBARA

Hiking: Santa Barbara Hikes,
www.santabarbarahikes.com/

Breweries: Central Coast Brewers Guild,
www.centralcoastbrewersguild.com/

Visitor Amenities: Santa Barbara Tourism Site,
www.santabarbaraca.com/

VENTURA

Hiking: Ventura County Coast Hiking,
www.venturacountycoast.com/hiking-in-ventura-county-coast/

Breweries: Central Coast Brewers Guild,
www.centralcoastbrewersguild.com/

Visitor Amenities: Visit Ventura,
www.visitventuraca.com/

LOS ANGELES

Hiking: Modern Hiker Best Hikes in Los Angeles,
www.modernhiker.com/best-hikes-in-los-angeles/

Breweries: Los Angeles County Brewers Guild,
www.labrewersguild.org/

Visitor Amenities: Discover Los Angeles,
www.discoverlosangeles.com/business

SAN BERNARDINO

Hiking: Komoot Hiking in San Bernardino County,
www.komoot.com/guide/1807239/hiking-in-san-bernardino-county

Breweries: Inland Empire Brewers Guild,
www.iebrewersguild.org/

Visitor Amenities: Discover Inland Empire,
www.discoverie.com

RIVERSIDE

Hiking: AllTrails,
www.alltrails.com/us/california/riverside

Breweries: Inland Empire Brewers Guild,
www.iebrewersguild.org/

Visitor Amenities: Discover Inland Empire,
www.discoverie.com

ORANGE

Hiking: OC Parks & Trails,
www.ocparks.com/parks-trails

Breweries: Orange County Brewers Guild,
www.ocbrewers.org/

Visitor Amenities: Visit California Orange County,
www.visitcalifornia.com/region/orange-county/

SAN DIEGO

Hiking: Hiking San Diego County,
www.hikingsdcounty.com/

Breweries: San Diego County Brewers Guild,
www.sdbeer.com/

Visitor Amenities: San Diego Tourism Authority,
www.sandiego.org/

TRAIL ETIQUETTE

The popularity of hiking today is at an all-time high, with outdoors-lovers of all experience levels hitting the trails. With Southern California's over 23 million residents and over twice that many annual visitors, it's easy for the more popular trails to get overwhelmed. This book includes a few of those popular trails along with local favorites and a number of lesser-known gems.

Regardless of your trail choice, there are some common courtesy practices that all hikers should follow to minimize our impact on the trails and be good stewards for the environment. These guidelines (roughly following the Leave No Trace principles, www.lnt.org) will help us all coexist safely and happily in a sustainable manner.

- **Stay on the trail.** Staying on the trail not only keeps you safe but also protects the environment by reducing erosion, keeping the trail the proper width, and protecting native plants.
- **Pack out trash.** Pack your trash back in your bag. If you need, carry a plastic bag with you to store your garbage (and trash previously left on the trail).
- **Leave nature as you found it.** Leave nature as undisturbed as possible. As they say, "Take only pictures, leave only footprints."
- **Respect wildlife.** Never feed wild animals. Expecting food from humans can mean that some larger predators have to be relocated or even euthanized.
- **Limit group size.** Some parks have cap sizes of ten to twelve people. Especially on narrow trails, groups larger than that can be hard on the environment and negatively impact other hikers. If you do have a larger group, consider splitting up into several smaller groups for the hike and reserving an appropriate picnic site where everyone can socialize afterwards.
- **Practice good bathroom hygiene.** When nature calls, know how to poop and pee in the woods with the least environmental impact—at least 200 feet away from the trail and any water source. Bury poop in an appropriately deep cathole and carry out your toilet paper.
- **Yield to uphill hikers and horses.** Hikers going uphill and horses have right of way on the trails. If you need to pause, move entirely off the trail so others can pass. Mountain bikers are technically supposed to yield to hikers, but sometimes it's not easy for them to do so. When that's the case, be friendly and yield.
- **Be considerate of others.** Everyone on the trail is here to enjoy time outside, so be considerate. Greet other trail-goers kindly. Enjoy the sounds of nature and let others do the same by keeping voices and noises low.
- **Park responsibly at the trailhead.** If the trailhead is full, consider returning later or postponing the hike to another day.

2

MAP & INDEX

MAP

BAKERSFIELD

SAN LUIS OBISPO

SANTA BARBARA

VENTURA

395

KERN

15

40

LOS ANGELES

SAN BERNARDINO

LOS ANGELES

ORANGE

RIVERSIDE

SAN DIEGO

Pacific Ocean

MEXICO

16 17 19 20 18 22 21 10 28 23 24 10 29 5 30 31 26 25 1 32 15 27 5 33 40 35 34 39 36 8 37 38

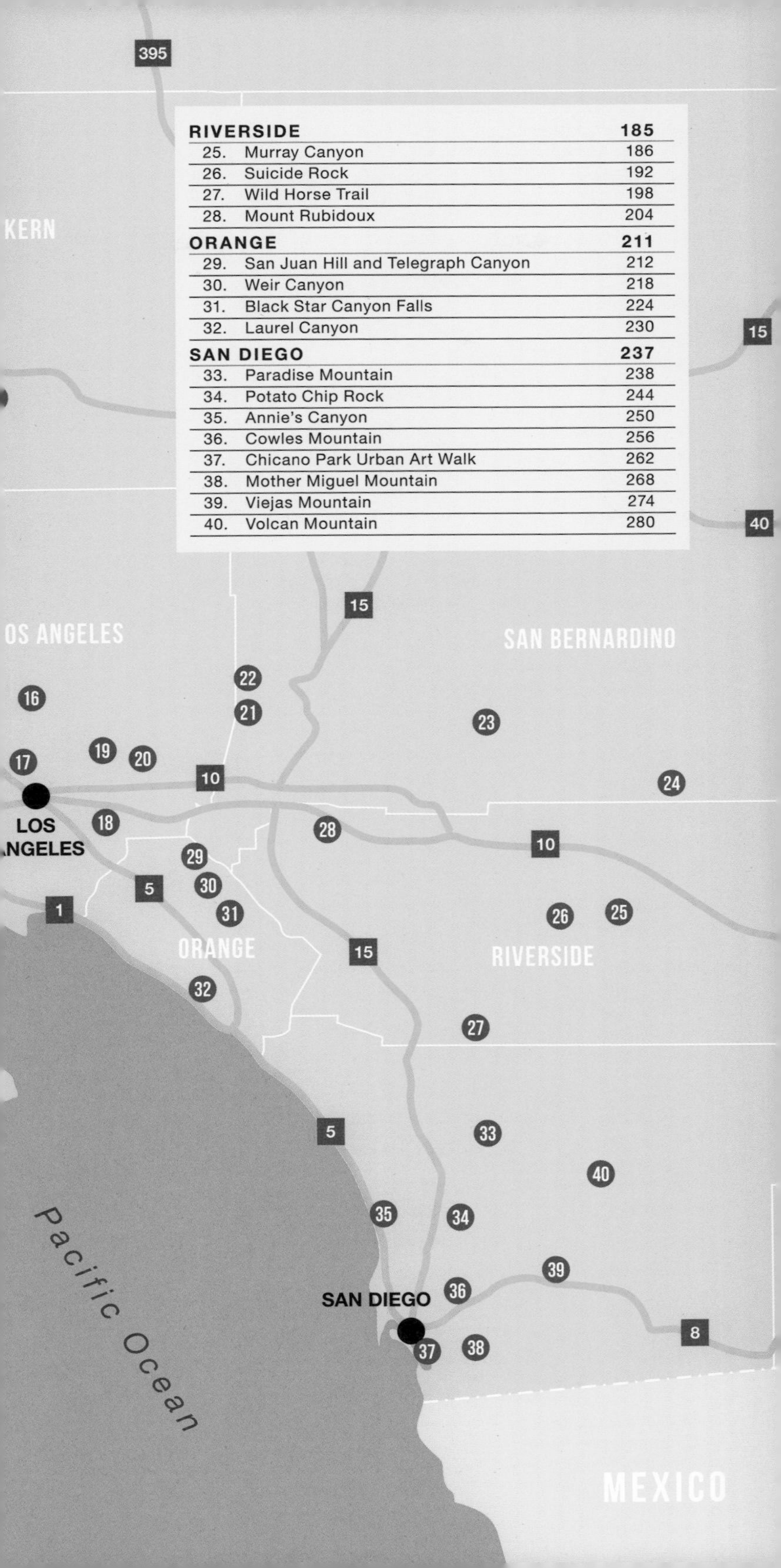

INDEX OF HIKES

BREWERIES & BEERS

BREWERY	BEER	PAGE
8 Bit Brewing Company	Guardians of Sunlight Lager	198
All Points Brewing Company	Panoramic Porter	204
Big Bear Lake Brewing Company	Sidewinder Red Ale	172
Brewjería Company	Tomo La Flor Pale Ale	140
Central Coast Brewing	Lucky Day IPA	50
Chula Vista Brewery	Can't Touch This Imperial Red Ale	268
Claremont Craft Ales	Baldy Pilsner	160
COLD Coast Brewing Company	Brown Evolved Brown Ale	58
Divine Science Brewing	Particle Haze Hazy IPA	224
Draughtsmen Aleworks	Cereal Killer Pale Ale	70
Figueroa Mountain Brewing Company	Davy Brown Ale	64
Green Cheek Beer Company	DDH Radiant Beauty IPA	218
Hop Secret Brewing Company	Close Talker Lager	152
Idyllwild Brewpub	Lone Willow Dark Lager	192
Julian Beer Company	Elevation 5353 Cold IPA	280
Kern River Brewing Company	Lovely Raspberry Kettle Sour	30
Laguna Beach Beer Company	Tuava Guava Hefeweizen	230
Las Palmas	Table Petite Farmhouse Ale	186
Lincoln Beer Company	Railsplitter Red Ale	128
Local Craft Beer	Snob's IPA	36
Malibu Brewing Company	Hatch Green Chile Lager	110
Mcilhenney Brewing Company	Muntz Rye IPA	274
Mujeres Brew House	Buenas Vibras Blonde Ale	262
Naughty Pine Brewing Company	Sturdy-B Pilsner	96
Oak and Otter Brewing Company	Bishop Brown Ale	44
Ojai Valley Brewery	Chaparral Herb Ale	84
Paperback Brewing Company	Bunny with a Chainsaw Hazy IPA	134
Pappy and Harriet's/Coachella Valley Brewing Co.	Desert Citrus Wheat Beer	178
Pizza Port Ocean Beach	Swami's IPA	256
Pocock Brewing Company	Surfing Hippos Hazy IPA	122
Rincon Reservation Road Brewery	Tropical Oasis Blonde Ale	238
RT Rogers Brewing Company	The Gold Spinner's Hefeweizen	146
Santa Monica Brew Works	310 Stomped Lemonade Shandy	116
Second Chance Beer Company	Fluffy Tangerine Clouds Hazy IPA	244
Stereo Brewing Company	Wall of Sound Stout	212
Tavern Tomoko and Ladyface Brewery	Blind Ambition Belgian Dark Ale	104
Third Window Brewing Company	The Dark Lager	76
Topa Topa Brewing Company	California Nitro Pub Ale	90
Viewpoint Brewing Company	Penitent Man IPA	250
Wrightwood Brew Co.	Hazy IPA	166

25

3

THE BEER HIKES

KERN

POWERS PEAK

A BEAUTIFUL GATEWAY TO THE SIERRAS

KERNVILLE

▷⋯ STARTING POINT	⋯✕ DESTINATION
CANNELL MEADOW TRAILHEAD	**POWERS PEAK**
◻ BREWERY	▦ HIKE TYPE
KERN RIVER BREWING COMPANY	**STRENUOUS**
🐾 DOG FRIENDLY	📅 SEASON
YES	**OCTOBER–MAY**
$ FEES	🕐 DURATION
NONE	**6 HOURS**
⛰ MAP REFERENCE	↦ LENGTH
POSTED AT TRAILHEAD	**10.1 MILES** (ROUND TRIP)
🔍 HIGHLIGHTS	〰 ELEVATION GAIN
PEAK VIEWS, WILDFLOWERS	**3,084 FEET**

LOVELY RASPBERRY KETTLE SOUR

4.8 % ALCOHOL CONTENT

 HAZY BLUSH

RASPBERRY, TART

SOUR, RASPBERRY

BITTERNESS

SWEETNESS

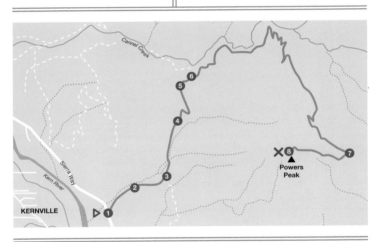

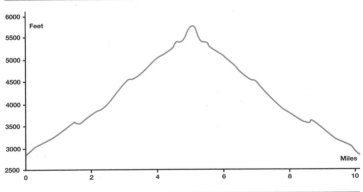

HIKE DESCRIPTION

Challenge yourself on this strenuous hike to a peak 5,778 feet above sea level with gorgeous mountain views and wildflowers. Afterwards, head down the road and reward yourself with a refreshing pint and fried pickles at the 100% employee-owned Kern River Brewing Co.

The northernmost location in this book, Kernville is primarily known for the Kern River and its whitewater rafting and kayaking, but the hiking trails offer spectacular scenery as well. Our trail showcases pristine wildlands in Sequoia National Forest, with views out to nearby Isabella Lake.

That said, you have to work for those views—the unrelenting elevation gain, high sun exposure, and a small section of mild scrambling make this hike a full-day adventure. From the trailhead, you'll set off up a mild incline on a dirt path through grassy meadows between two hills. The meadows are often brown, but for a few weeks around April the hillsides come alive with splashes of orange, yellow, white, and purple wildflowers. Skirting around the first hill on the right, you'll get a view of the rocky ridgeline and Powers Peak on the right (you'll be hiking around the backside of the mountain).

A little over a mile and a half in, you'll see Cannell Creek flowing to the left at the base of the valley. In every direction, you'll enjoy views of rolling mountains with granite rocks interspersed amid browned grass, dark green bushes, and pine and oak trees. Keep a close eye on the sandy-gravel trail, as you may see reptiles like Pacific rattlesnakes, California king snakes, western fence lizards, and Blainville's horned lizards. The Blainville's horned lizard is a native species with a flat,

oval-shaped body and spines from head to tail. Its coloring blends in remarkably well with the sand. If threatened, the horned lizard squirts a stream of blood from the corner of its eyes to distract or startle a potential predator.

Around four and a half miles in, you'll reach the saddle on the ridgeline. Here you'll turn off the Cannell Trail and head for Powers Peak. You'll gain approximately 500 feet over the next half mile, with gradients of up to 36 percent, climbing along a fallen tree and scrambling up some loose dirt. The trail flattens out slightly and weaves among waist-high shrubs like California lilacs before reaching the rocky summit. (Powers Peak is named after fifth-generation Kernville resident Robert L. "Bob" Powers, who wrote nine history books on the Kern River Valley.)

TURN-BY-TURN DIRECTIONS

1. From the small parking area, go through a gate and proceed on the 33E32 Cannell Meadow Trail.
2. At 0.3 miles, continue straight, ignoring a trail on the right.
3. At 0.6 miles, keep to the left as indicated by the wooden sign marked "TRAIL."
4. At 1.1 miles, keep right at the unmarked fork.
5. At 1.5 miles, pass through a metal gate and continue straight on the main trail.
6. At 1.6 miles, keep right on the 33E32 Trail.
7. At a T-junction marked with a metal post at 4.4 miles, keep right on a narrow trail going uphill.
8. At 5.0 miles, pass what looks like an old stone fireplace and reach Powers Peak, marked with a plaque honoring Bob Powers. Return the way you came.

FIND THE TRAILHEAD

From Bakersfield, take CA-58 E for 30.5 miles. Turn left onto Bealville Rd. towards Bealville and Caliente. Proceed for 2.0 miles to Caliente, at which point the road curves right and turns into Caliente Bodfish Rd. After 3.2 miles, turn left to stay on Caliente Bodfish Rd. Continue for 12.4 miles; then turn left to stay on Caliente Bodfish Rd. After 14.9 miles, you'll reach Bodfish; here, the road turns into Lake Isabella Blvd. After 2.9 miles, turn left onto Kernville Rd. Proceed for 0.3 miles and continue straight as the road turns into CA-155 W. Proceed on this main road for 11.0 miles and turn left on Buena Vista Dr. After 0.2 miles, turn left onto Sierra Way. The dirt pull-off will be on the right after 1.3 miles at a sign for the Cannell Trail.

KERN RIVER BREWING COMPANY

Founders Eric and Rebecca Giddens fell in love with Kernville while living in San Diego and traveling up to the Kern River for whitewater kayaking. Both Eric and Rebecca competed in the Olympics in canoe slalom, and Rebecca won a silver medal in the K-1 women's event in 2004 at the Athens Olympic Games. After these accomplishments, the couple moved to Kernville and opened the Kern River Brewing Company in 2005.

The brewery now has two locations next door to each other—the upper, original location has a rustic brewpub vibe with classic pub foods, while the lower site serves a variety of mac and cheeses, bowls, sandwiches, and flatbreads. The brewery was named "Best Brewery Group of the Year" in 2019 at the Great American Beer Festival, taking home two golds and two silvers. After over fifteen years of ownership, the Giddens transitioned the brewery to be 100-percent employee-owned to ensure that it continues to serve the community for years to come. The brewery is known for its award-winning IPAs, but after your 10-mile hike to Powers Peak, the tangy, light Lovely Raspberry Kettle Sour (named after the 19th-century miner Lovely Rogers) really hits the spot.

LAND MANAGER

Sequoia National Forest Kern River Ranger District
11380 Kernville Road
Kernville, CA 93238
(760) 376-3781
www.fs.usda.gov/recarea/sequoia/recreation/recarea/?recid=79571
Map: www.fs.usda.gov/Internet/FSE_DOCUMENTS/stelprd3800325.jpg

BREWERY/RESTAURANT

Kern River Brewing Company
13415 Sierra Way
Kernville, CA 93238
(760) 376-2337
www.kernriverbrewing.com/

Distance from trailhead: 1.3 miles

WIND TURBINES PCT SEGMENT

HIKE A PORTION OF THE 2,650-MILE PACIFIC CREST TRAIL

MOJAVE

▷··· STARTING POINT	···✗ DESTINATION
TEHACHAPI WILLOW SPRINGS RD/ CAMERON CANYON RD	**WIND TURBINES VIEWPOINT**
🍺 BREWERY	HIKE TYPE
LOCAL CRAFT BEER	**MODERATE**
🐾 DOG FRIENDLY	📅 SEASON
YES	**YEAR-ROUND**
💲 FEES	🕐 DURATION
NONE	**3 HOURS**
🗺 MAP REFERENCE	↦ LENGTH
PACIFIC CREST TRAIL ASSOCIATION	**7.9 MILES** (ROUND TRIP)
🔎 HIGHLIGHTS	〰 ELEVATION GAIN
PCT TRAIL, WILDFLOWERS, WINDMILLS	**1,457 FEET**

SNOB'S IPA

6.9% ALCOHOL CONTENT

STRAW

GRAPEFRUIT

CRISP, STONE FRUIT

BITTERNESS

SWEETNESS

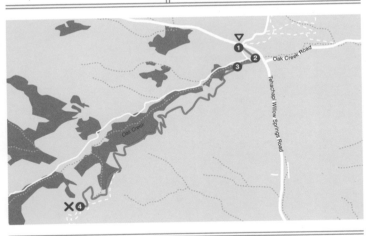

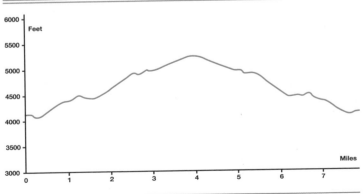

HIKE DESCRIPTION

Get a taste of hiking the famous Pacific Crest Trail (PCT) on this 7.9-mile route through hundreds of wind turbines and desert wildflowers. Afterwards, taste a crisp West Coast IPA from Local Craft Beer.

The PCT is a long-distance "thru-hiking" trail running up the West Coast of the United States from Mexico to Canada. The most common way of hiking the trail is to take it northbound, starting at the border with Mexico anytime from early spring to mid-May. Our section of the trail gets the most hikers in April, May, and June, so if you're hiking during the spring, expect to see some thru-hikers who have already notched around 550 miles!

The beauty of hiking along the PCT is that you can go as far as you want. The trail continues with or without you, so there isn't a distinct turn-around point. This almost 4-mile section leads you through rolling hills and past windmills, wildflowers, and a few Joshua trees.

At the parking area, you'll see a BLM (Bureau of Land Management) sign for "Pacific Crest National Scenic Trail, Desert Segment." You'll follow the singletrack dirt trail southeast through low desert scrub grass. In every direction, you'll see towering white windmills dotting the hillsides.

This area, known as Tehachapi Pass, is often considered the birthplace of wind energy and has one of the largest wind farms in the world. The pass is particularly attractive for wind energy for two reasons: one, its proximity to Los Angeles—so the energy doesn't have to travel too far—and two, it's a natural wind channel directing high-speed winds from the Pacific Ocean into the Mojave Desert. There are over 5,000 wind turbines here, ranging from 45 to 300 feet tall.

As you set out on the trail and gradually gain elevation, you'll get a progressively better view of the expansive wind farm stretching over the rolling hills. The trail mostly traverses a hillside with a consistent uphill gradient, zigzagging along the edge of a drop-off on the right. The singletrack dirt trail is easy to follow and well marked with PCT stickers on metal poles. Traversing along the hillside rather than heading directly up, it's easy to write off how much of the trail is uphill.

At over 5,000 feet above sea level, this area is considered "high desert." Through most of the year, it is hot, dry, and sunny. However, after a rainy winter or spring, the trail is surrounded by blooming wildflowers such as lupin, fiddleneck, and California poppy. Around halfway to the turnaround point, you'll walk through a cluster of Joshua trees, which look like they belong in a Dr. Seuss book. Joshua trees aren't actually trees; they're succulents of the agave family and a keystone species in the Mojave Desert, providing essential habitats and food for other species in the ecosystem like Yucca Moths, cactus wrens, and desert night lizards. With climate change making the deserts hotter and drier, Joshua trees may struggle to survive.

Around three and a half miles in, you'll hit a series of bends in the trail. After these curves will be our stopping point (though you're welcome to go further). Looking west further down the trail, the Tehachapi and Sierra Nevada mountains gradually get more dramatic. Looking northwest in the direction you just came from, you'll see the foothills and full glory of the windmills stretching out below.

TURN-BY-TURN DIRECTIONS

1. From the large dirt parking area, cross the street and follow the signs for the PCT.

2. At 0.2 miles, reach a picnic table with information provided by the local PCT trail angels (people helping thru-hikers), and often a water supply. The water is for PCT hikers—please bring your own and don't take theirs! Continue past the table, crossing a small bridge; then pass through a metal gate on the right with a sticker for the PCT.

3. At 0.5 miles, cross an unmarked dirt road and continue straight along the singletrack trail.

4. At 4.0 miles, after curving around a hill, turn back and return the way you came.

FIND THE TRAILHEAD

From the center of Tehachapi, head south on South Curry St. After 1.6 miles, turn left onto Highline Rd.; proceed for 3.1 miles and then turn right onto Tehachapi Willow Springs Rd. After 5.4 miles, reach Cameron Canyon Rd. on the left. The trailhead is at this intersection. On the right of Tehachapi Willow Springs Rd., you'll find a small dirt parking area. There's a larger parking area across the road which you can access by turning left onto Cameron Canyon Rd. and then immediately right.

LOCAL CRAFT BEER

Palmdale-based couple Tyson and Katie Southworth bought Honey Wagon Brewing in 2015. The couple kept the name for a year, then changed it to Local Craft Beer (often simply LCB) in 2016 on their first anniversary. Tyson, the mastermind behind many of LCB's recipes, started homebrewing in 2006 when Katie, who's a huge beer fan, bought him a kit so he could make her beer. From here, the enterprise snowballed into a fully-fledged brewery.

Now, the couple works with lead brewer Joey Lewis, who started as a home brewer and has worked his way up the ranks at LCB over the years. The close-knit team specializes in IPAs and "slurshies," which are slushy-style fruited beers. While the mom-and-pop shop is small and local with an eight-barrel brewhouse and thirty-barrel fermenters, the brewery is fully international, shipping to places like China, the Netherlands, Spain, and France.

The team likes to continually change recipes and create different beers, but Snob's IPA is the brewery's flagship, a West Coast IPA that's regularly on tap. It's light and crisp for a West Coast IPA, with grapefruit and stone-fruit tasting notes.

LAND MANAGER

Pacific Crest Trail Association
2150 River Plaza Drive, Suite 155
Sacramento, CA 95833
(916) 285-1846
www.pcta.org/
Map: www.pcta.org/discover-the-trail/maps/

BREWERY/RESTAURANT

Local Craft Beer
365 Enterprise Way G
Tehachapi, CA 93561
(661) 822-2337
www.localcraftbeer.net/

Distance from trailhead: 10.7 miles

SAN LUIS OBISPO

BISHOP PEAK

HIKE TO THE HIGHEST VOLCANIC PEAK OF THE MORROS

SAN LUIS OBISPO

▷··· STARTING POINT	···✗ DESTINATION
PATRICIA STREET TRAILHEAD	**BISHOP PEAK**
🍺 BREWERY	🔲 HIKE TYPE
OAK AND OTTER BREWING COMPANY	**MODERATE** 🚶
🐾 DOG FRIENDLY	📅 SEASON
YES (LEASH REQUIRED)	**YEAR-ROUND**
$ FEES	🕐 DURATION
NONE	**2 HOURS**
🗺 MAP REFERENCE	↦ LENGTH
POSTED AT TRAILHEAD	**4 MILES** (ROUND TRIP)
🔍 HIGHLIGHTS	〰 ELEVATION GAIN
PANORAMIC VIEWS, VOLCANIC HISTORY	**1,184 FT**

BISHOP BROWN ALE

COFFEE BROWN

FRUITY

CHOCOLATE,
NUTTY,
CARAMEL

BITTERNESS	SWEETNESS

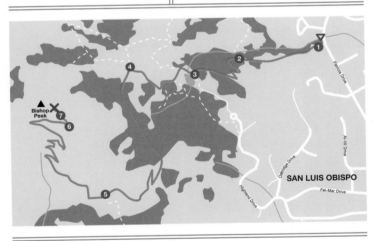

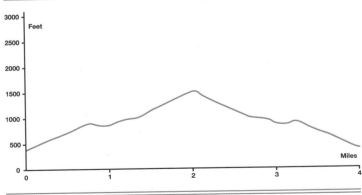

HIKE DESCRIPTION

Hike to the top of the tallest of the Nine Sisters volcanic peaks (aka Morros) for a strenuous but rewarding workout with panoramic views. Then, head to Oak and Otter for a celebratory brew named after the peak you just climbed.

At 1,546 feet, Bishop Peak is the highest summit of the volcanic range that extends from San Luis Obispo to Morro Bay. The Bishop Peak Trail offers a steep challenge along with stunning views of the entire mountain range and out to the ocean. The hike is especially good for sunset views but can be very hot in the summer because there isn't much shade.

The Bishop Peak Trail is the most popular hike in San Luis Obispo, so be prepared to share the trail with other hikers, especially if you're going on a weekend. There's ample street parking at the trailhead but no designated parking and spaces can fill up on weekends. If this happens, there are two other nearby trailhead entrances on Highland Drive and Foothill Road that lead to the Bishop Peak Trail as well.

The hike starts on a wide, partially paved path, but soon you'll be on a small, steep dirt trail switchbacking through oak trees. The trail emerges from the trees to an open clearing with a view of Bishop Peak looming above. After a short section following a wide trail up a grassy slope towards the peak, you'll find yourself under a mix of oak and bay trees. The path stays relatively flat here while winding close to the rocky cliff base. As the trail circles around the mountain, you'll come out of the forest and tackle steep switchbacks along a rocky singletrack path with many large orange boulders among coastal sage scrub plants like black sage, coyote brush, and deerweed. At midday, with direct sun exposure, this can be especially challenging, but you'll come upon progressively more rewarding views of the surrounding hills and the city of San Luis Obispo as you approach the rocky summit.

The Bishop Peak Natural Area hosts some of the best local climbing routes, so don't be surprised if you see climbers scaling nearby rocks as you hike.

TURN-BY-TURN DIRECTIONS

1. From the trailhead on Patricia Drive, pass a gate and start off on the wide dirt path headed uphill, following the blue arrows for the Summit Trail.
2. At 0.2 miles, after a short stretch of pavement, take a left onto an unmarked narrow trail.
3. At 0.5 miles, after a series of switchbacks, the trail joins a wider path near a seasonal cattle pond. Take a right onto the main trail, passing a large interpretive display. Ahead, take a left and two rights following blue arrows for the Summit Trail, passing a water tank on the left
4. At 0.7 miles, after passing through a green cattle gate, take a sharp left on the signed Bishop Peak Trail. Head into a short section of shaded forest and pass a small rock-climbing access trail on the right.
5. At 1.3 miles, reach a fork and stay right, heading uphill.
6. At 1.9 miles, after following the trail around the side of the hill and taking a series of steep switchbacks, visit a lookout point on the right for a view of San Luis Obispo below and nearby Madonna Peak on the right. Return to the main trail after admiring the view.
7. At 2.0 miles, a gray bench with the words "end of trail" etched into the side marks the end of the established trail. Optional scrambling on sandstone boulders on either side leads to full panoramic views. From here, return to the trailhead the way you came.

FIND THE TRAILHEAD

From San Luis Obispo, head northwest on Santa Rosa Street. The street eventually turns into Highway 1 North/Cabrillo Highway. 1.4 miles from the turn onto Santa Rosa Street, turn left on Highland Drive. After 0.6 miles, turn right onto Patricia Drive. The trailhead with its three-paneled interpretive display will be on the left side after 0.5 miles. Street parking is available.

OAK AND OTTER BREWING COMPANY

This small-batch taproom is a recent (January 2020) addition to the SLO brewery scene. Head brewer Dylan Roddick took over and renamed the Seven Sisters brewery, giving the interior a stylish remodel but keeping the friendly vibes and favorite brews like Bishop Brown, Islay Peak IPA, and Black Hill stout—all named after volcanic peaks in the area. With ten years of homebrewing experience and several home-brewing competition medals, Roddick specializes in English-style dark ales, stouts, and porters including Bishop Brown, which has a nutty and chocolatey taste with a smooth caramel finish.

LAND MANAGER

San Luis Obispo Open Spaces
990 Palm Street
San Luis Obispo, CA 93401
(805) 781-7302
https://www.slocity.org/government/department-directory/
parks-and-recreation/ranger-service#ad-image-0
Map: https://www.slocity.org/home/showdocument?id=16660

BREWERY/RESTAURANT

Oak and Otter Brewing Co.
181 Tank Farm Rd #110
San Luis Obispo, CA 93401
(805) 439-2529
http://www.oakandotterbrewing.com/

Distance from trailhead: 6.2 miles

POINT BUCHON

HIKE ALONG COASTAL HEADLANDS AND VIEW A SINKHOLE

LOS OSOS

▷⋯ STARTING POINT	⋯✕ DESTINATION
POINT BUCHON TRAILHEAD PARKING	**COASTAL OVERLOOK**
🍺 BREWERY	🗺 HIKE TYPE
CENTRAL COAST BREWING	**EASY** 🚶
🐾 DOG FRIENDLY	📅 SEASON
NO	**YEAR-ROUND**
$ FEES	🕐 DURATION
NONE	**3 HOURS**
⛰ MAP REFERENCE	↦ LENGTH
POSTED AT TRAILHEAD	**7.5 MILES** (ROUND TRIP)
🔍 HIGHLIGHTS	〰 ELEVATION GAIN
SINKHOLE, MARINE WILDLIFE, WILDFLOWERS	**646 FT**

LUCKY DAY IPA

DEEP,
CLEAR GOLD

CITRUS,
TROPICAL FRUIT

HOPPY,
CITRUS

BITTERNESS

SWEETNESS

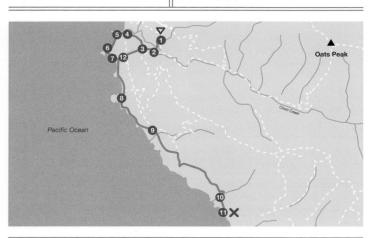

Oats Peak

Pacific Ocean

Coon Creek

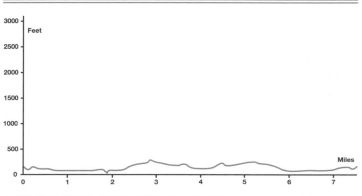

HIKE DESCRIPTION

Hike along well-preserved coastline and scan the horizon for whale spouts, dolphins, sea otters, and harbor seals. Then head back to San Luis Obispo for a refreshing brew at Central Coast Brewing's Higuera Street location.

Tucked in on the northern end of Pacific Gas & Electric (PG&E) property and just south of Montaña de Oro State Park, the Point Buchon and Pecho Coast area has over 10,000 years of human history. It was first inhabited by the Native American Northern Chumash people, who used the native plants and animals for food, medicine, and raw materials. When the Spanish came into the area and developed Mission San Luis Obispo de Tolosa in 1772, it dramatically impacted the Northern Chumash people's way of life, and they were eventually pushed off the land.

The name "Point Buchon" honors a prominent Northern Chumash leader from the mid-18th century. PG&E works with Northern Chumash people today to preserve the land's natural beauty and history. Walking along this shoreline path, you'll find twelve different interpretive displays dotting the trail. Read about many salient aspects of the area, from the history of the Northern Chumash people to the causes of a large sinkhole that collapsed in the 1990s, which you'll see about 0.7 miles into the hike.

You'll probably see a variety of marine wildlife on this hike, and there's a wide variety of flora and fauna to see on land as well. Cows pasture here year-round, while in the spring, the fields are full of California poppies, goldfields, blue dicks, and other wildflowers. Plus, look out for wildlife like bobcats, coyotes, badgers, peregrine falcons, and golden eagles.

TURN-BY-TURN DIRECTIONS

1. From the parking lot, follow the paved road that heads south to a chain link fence.
2. At 0.2 miles, stop at the check-in station to sign in; then stay right and start down the dirt and gravel trail, following signs for the Point Buchon Trail.
3. At 0.3 miles, keep right at the fork.
4. At 0.6 miles, continue straight towards the coastal cliff-edge. (Optional: a pathway on the right leads to a small beach area.)
5. At 0.7 miles, reach the sinkhole with a wooden fence around it.
6. At 1.0 miles, take the right path to Point Buchon for a nice coastline view.
7. At 1.2 miles, reach Point Buchon. Circle back to the main path and then veer right towards an overlook with a bench and path intersection. At the intersection, keep right to continue further along the headland following signs for the Point Buchon Trail. For a shorter hike, take the left path to loop back to the check-in station.
8. At 1.8 miles, reach Disney Point lookout.
9. At the intersection at 2.4 miles, keep right following the Point Buchon Trail; at the fork approximately 600 feet further on, take the left path to remain on the Point Buchon Trail.
10. At 3.8 miles, cross a wider dirt road and continue straight along the trail (unmarked).
11. At 4.0 miles, reach a bench at the clearly signposted end point. Turn around here and follow the same trail back.
12. At the intersection at 6.9 miles, just before Point Buchon, veer slightly right towards the check-in/out station.

FIND THE TRAILHEAD

From San Luis Obispo, take Los Osos Valley Road for 8.4 miles into Los Osos. This road turns into Pecho Valley Road. Stay on Pecho Valley Road for the next 5 miles as it becomes smaller, winding through coastal bluffs and the Montaña de Oro State Park. Pass four parking lots in Montaña de Oro and park in the last lot at the end of the road, where you'll see two pit toilets and picnic tables.

CENTRAL COAST BREWING

Central Coast Brewing has been a staple of the San Luis Obisbo beer scene since its first location opened 25 years ago on Monterey Street in downtown SLO under founder George Peterson. The Higuera Street venue has a slightly more upscale, classic feel and is now the brewery's primary location. Here, you can grab a pint while sitting next to the very tanks that brewed your drink. With its 24 taps, the brewery offers a wide selection of different beers, from classic IPAs to a

raspberry sour and a peanut butter stout. One of the flagship brews, the Lucky Day IPA, is a hop-lovers dream with an upfront bitterness and citrusy hop flavor. The beer won a World Beer Cup Gold in 2016 and GABF Bronze in 2018. For an extra-refreshing posthike drink, ask about the beer slushies.

LAND MANAGER

Pacific Gas and Electric (PG&E)
Pecho Valley Road
Montaña de Oro State Park
Los Osos, CA 93402
(805) 528-8758
www.pge.com/en_US/residential/in-your-community/local-environment/diablo-canyon-trails/point-buchon-trail.page
Map: www.pge.com/pge_global/local/images/data/en-us/
in-your-community/local-environment/diablo-canyon-trails/map_
point_buchon_trail.jpg

BREWERY/RESTAURANT

Central Coast Brewing
6 Higuera St.
San Luis Obispo, CA 93401
(805) 783-2739
www.centralcoastbrewing.com/

Distance from trailhead: 16.8 miles

SANTA BARBARA

LA PURÍSIMA MISSION STATE HISTORIC PARK

EXPLORE CALIFORNIA'S BEST-RESTORED MISSION

LOMPOC

▷⋯ STARTING POINT	⋯✕ DESTINATION
LA PURÍSIMA MISSION VISITOR CENTER	**MISSION BUILDINGS**
🍺 BREWERY	HIKE TYPE
COLD COAST BREWING COMPANY	**EASY**
🐾 DOG FRIENDLY	SEASON
YES (LEASH REQUIRED)	**YEAR-ROUND**
$ FEES	🕐 DURATION
YES (CALIFORNIA EXPLORER PASS)	**2 HOURS 15 MIN.**
⌖ MAP REFERENCE	↦ LENGTH
POSTED AT TRAILHEAD/ IN VISITOR CENTER	**4.5 MILES** (LOOP)
🔎 HIGHLIGHTS	〰 ELEVATION GAIN
1820S MISSION, WILDFLOWERS	**226 FEET**

6.6 %
ALCOHOL CONTENT

BROWN EVOLVED
BROWN ALE

 CHOCOLATE BROWN

 CHOCOLATE, MALTY

 MALTY, RICH

BITTERNESS

SWEETNESS

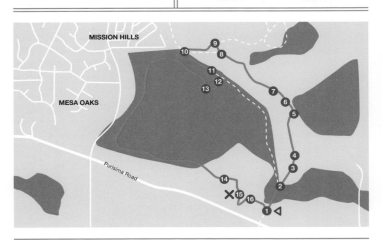

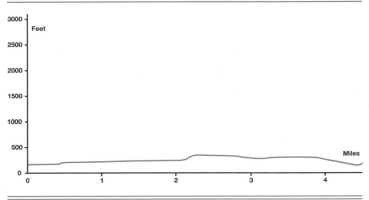

HIKE DESCRIPTION

Delve into the past and learn what life was like in California in the 1820s at La Purísima Mission State Historic Park. Afterwards, head to today's local hangout for an award-winning brown ale at COLD Coast Brewing Co.

The Misión la Purísima Concepción de María Santísima was founded on Immaculate Conception Day (December 8th) in 1787. Today, it is the best restored of California's twenty-one historic missions. It once covered almost 300,000 acres of land that had originally been inhabited by Native Americans. The California missions are often considered a key piece of Californian history—a complex history due to the many and terrible injustices done to Native Americans. Today, the park spans 2,000 acres and boasts 25 miles of trails.

You'll see a modern-looking visitor center to the right of the parking lot; here you can pop in for a map, learn more about the history of the park, and use the restroom. The trail sets out from the parking lot on a wide dirt road. It's mostly flat, leading through a mix of oak trees and bushes like sagebrush and coyote brush. Around a half-mile in, you'll come upon a small adobe structure on the left with an interpretive display. This was the Spring House and contained the mission's water filtration system. You can go inside the building and observe how the water passes through sand to be filtered. The water then traveled through clay pipes underground to the center fountain for general use.

After walking on the wide trail for just under half a mile, you'll veer off on a narrow trail under oak trees and reach the next stop: a wide pit lined with adobe brick with a shallow channel for water. This was the

mission's tanning vat, where hides soaked for months in water and crushed oak bark, which released tannic acid.

You'll follow the main trail to a wide concrete hole on the right; this was part of the mission's aqueduct that stored and transported water. Walking around the hole, you'll briefly diverge off the main trail onto a more concealed path leading through a natural tunnel of twisted oak trees. When this trail begins to loop back towards the visitor center, you'll veer onto a small, overgrown trail leading up a short but steep hill through sage bushes and oak trees.

You'll emerge onto a wide dirt trail lined with sage, fiddleneck, and occasional oak and pine trees. Following this trail, you'll eventually head back downhill and wind up directly behind and above the main mission structures. After descending and circling around to the front of the mission, you can take your time exploring the ten restored buildings, fully furnished as they would have been in the 1820s and including a weaving room, blacksmithing building, sleeping quarters, and dining area. When you're ready, head back to the parking lot.

TURN-BY-TURN DIRECTIONS

1. From the visitor center and parking lot, take the wide unmarked dirt road leading behind two adobe buildings.
2. At 0.2 miles, keep right on the wide unmarked dirt road next to a wooden fence enclosure.
3. At 0.3 miles, ignore a trail on either side and continue straight on the Las Zanjas Trail.
4. At 0.4 miles, reach the Spring House La Casa del Manatial on the left.
5. At 0.8 miles, turn right onto the El Noque Trail. Around 300 feet later, you'll reach the tanning vat directly to the left of the trail. From here, turn back and return to the Las Zanjas Trail; turn right and continue.
6. At 1.0 miles, reach the aqueduct on the right. Go around the aqueduct to a slightly hidden upper trail on the right.
7. At 1.1 miles, meet the Las Zanjas Trail again and continue straight.
8. At 1.5 miles, keep to the right on the wide, sandy, unmarked road.
9. At 1.6 miles, keep left on a wide unmarked trail which circles back towards the Las Zanjas Trail.
10. At 1.8 miles, reach an intersection with three trails; follow the middle, unmarked option (this is the historic El Camino Real), passing a wooden bench with three crosses engraved on it.
11. At 2.0 miles, turn right onto the El Chaparral Trail.
12. At 2.1 miles, ignore an unmarked intersecting path and continue straight on the more obvious unmarked El Chaparral Trail leading uphill.
13. At 2.2 miles, emerge onto the Cuclillo de Tierra Trail and turn right. Continue on this dirt road, ignoring all other side trails.
14. At 4.0 miles, reach a paved road; cross the road and take a small, unmarked sandy trail. Continue on this, ignoring smaller trail spurs.
15. At 4.2 miles, reach the back of the main mission buildings. Follow the trail downhill, circling around the mission, and then turn left and arrive at the front of the mission.
16. Explore the mission buildings as much as you'd like and when you're ready, follow the main path leading away from the buildings and back to the parking lot.

FIND THE TRAILHEAD

From Santa Barbara, take US-101 N/CA-1 N (Highway 1 or the "PCH") for 34.6 miles until US-101 N and CA-1 N diverge at Exit 132. Here, take the exit for CA-1 towards Lompoc and Vandenberg SFB. At the end of the off-ramp, turn left onto CA-1 N; proceed for 17.9 miles. When CA-1 hits a T-junction with CA-246, turn right onto CA-246 E. After 1.8 miles, turn left onto Mission Gate Rd. You'll start seeing signs for "Mission La Purísima"—follow these signs and arrows. After 0.4 miles, cross Purísima Rd. and reach the parking lot.

COLD COAST BREWING COMPANY

While this part of Southern California is notably temperate and often "cold," the cold in COLD Coast Brewing Company is actually an acronym for the last names of the four founders: David (Dave) Caro, Eric Oviatt, Michael (Mike) Lamping, and Jason Drew. All locals who grew up in the Lompoc area, the group of four (and their families) opened the brewery in 2022 as a place for the community to come together and enjoy good beer. The brewery does not have a kitchen, in part because the owners feel it serves the community better as a large gathering space where people can bring outside food and avoid the logistical challenges of large restaurant reservations. However, it does have regular local food trucks outside. Mike and Eric, who started homebrewing about seven years ago, both work at the brewery full-time, with Mike doing most of the brewing while Eric—who got his brewer's certificate from UCSD—manages the recipes, purchasing, and logistical work.

In their first year of operation, the team won a bronze medal at the Great American Beer Festival for Brown Evolved, a spin-off of their original brown ale. Brown Evolved is rich and flavorful, with the textbook balance of hops and malt that you'd expect from an American brown ale.

LAND MANAGER

La Purísima Mission State Historic Park
2295 Purísima Rd.
Lompoc, CA 93436
(805) 733-3713
www.parks.ca.gov/?page_id=598
Map: www.healthypeoplehealthytrails.org/maps/mission-la-purisima-loop-trail.pdf

BREWERY/RESTAURANT

COLD Coast Brewing Company
118 W Ocean Ave.
Lompoc, CA 93436
(805) 819-0723
www.coldcoastbrewing.com/

Distance from trailhead: 3.6 miles

FIGUEROA MOUNTAIN

HIKE TO A MOUNTAIN LOOKOUT WITH 360-DEGREE VIEWS

LOS OLIVOS

▷⋯ STARTING POINT	⋯✗ DESTINATION
FOREST SERVICE RD 8N16	**FIGUEROA MOUNTAIN**
🍺 BREWERY	HIKE TYPE
FIGUEROA MOUNTAIN BREWING COMPANY	**MODERATE**
🐾 DOG FRIENDLY	📅 SEASON
YES	**YEAR-ROUND**
$ FEES	🕐 DURATION
NO	**1 HOUR 50 MIN.**
🗺 MAP REFERENCE	↦ LENGTH
FIGUEROA MOUNTAIN RECREATION AREA	**4.1 MILES** (ROUND TRIP)
🔍 HIGHLIGHTS	〰 ELEVATION GAIN
SUMMIT VIEWS, WILDFLOWERS	**948 FEET**

DAVY BROWN ALE

 DARK BROWN

 MOCHA, MALT

 THICK, COFFEE

BITTERNESS

SWEETNESS

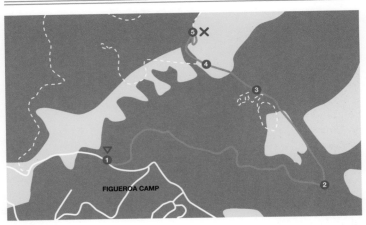

FIGUEROA CAMP

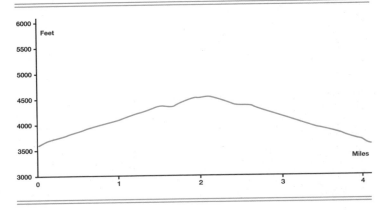

HIKE DESCRIPTION

Hike to the peak of Figueroa Mountain for panoramic summit views of the San Rafael Mountains. Afterward, head to Figueroa Mountain Brewing Co. and indulge in a Davy Brown Ale.

At 4,534 feet above sea level, Figueroa Mountain—or, as the locals fondly call it, "Fig Mountain"—is the sixth-highest peak in the San Rafael Mountains and the highest in the northern section of the range. Fig Mountain was named after José Figueroa, who was the governor of Alta California from 1833 to 1835 and wrote the first book published in California, titled *The Manifesto To The Mexican Republic*. The trail up to Fig Mountain is a forest service road and is technically drivable, but it's closed to cars in wet conditions and is a notably bumpy ride even in good conditions. Still, you may see some four-wheel-drive vehicles on the trail. While sharing the trail with cars can be a nuisance, the views and vibrant wildflowers along the road still make it well worth hiking.

From start to peak, the trail is almost entirely uphill, first traversing a hillside and then looping back to the summit. The service road starts out under pine and oak trees among shrubs and seasonal wildflowers. While the hike is definitely a workout, it offers various overlook points on the way up that increasingly reward you for your efforts. For the first mile, the road climbs steadily along the south side of the mountain with dispersed shade coverage. Between breaks in the trees, you'll enjoy views looking over Los Olivos and the Santa Ynez Valley.

Around a mile in, you'll reach the ridgeline leading to Fig Mountain. Rounding a corner, you'll finish the hike along the other side of the ridge. This section of the trail offers an entirely different view; you're now on the northeast side of the mountain looking at the San Rafael Mountains extending out to the horizon. As you climb higher, the oak trees give way to more pine trees and, in the spring, an abundance of lupin and California poppies.

Soon after passing the Pino Alto Nature Trail and picnic area, you'll reach the summit. Here you can take in the views in all their glory and circle around the lookout tower. (The current concrete version was built in 1965 to replace the original wooden structure from 1923.) The lookout was constructed as a viewpoint to watch for wildfires. Today, it's occasionally used to monitor lightning strikes but is not regularly staffed.

For the best views, go at sunset—but check the brewery's hours to make sure you'll get back in time for a pint!

TURN-BY-TURN DIRECTIONS

1. From the trailhead, go up the main service road in the direction of Pino Alto, Lookout, and Cumbre.
2. At 1.1 miles, follow a hairpin left turn on the main dirt road; ignore a trail spur going off the main road on the right.
3. At 1.6 miles, reach the Pino Alto picnic area and nature trail and continue straight along the dirt road.
4. At 1.8 miles, keep right on Figueroa Lookout Road in the direction of Figueroa Lookout and Figueroa Vista Point.
5. At 2.0 miles, reach Figueroa Lookout Point. Take your time exploring around the lookout building on all sides of the peak to fully enjoy the view. Return the way you came.

FIND THE TRAILHEAD

From Santa Barbara, take US-101 N. After 4.2 miles, take Exit 101B for State St. towards Cachuma Lake and CA-154. At the end of the off-ramp, continue straight on Calle Real. After 0.3 miles, turn right onto CA-154; stay on CA-154 for 29.2 miles. When you get into Los Olivos, turn right onto Figueroa Mountain Rd. Part of the enjoyment of this trail is driving up winding Figueroa Mountain Rd. with its many vistas, so take your time! After 13.0 miles, Forest Service Rd. 8N16 will be on the left heading uphill. You can park at the pull-out in front of the road. If this is full, double back 0.3 miles to additional parking in a pull-out for Zaca Ridge Rd.

FIGUEROA MOUNTAIN BREWING COMPANY

Father-and-son duo Jim and Jaime Dietenhofer opened Figueroa Mountain Brewing Co. in 2010 in nearby Buellton. Jaime had been try-ing to persuade Jim to open a brewery with him for years, and Jim finally gave in. Jaime grew up with a view of Fig Mountain from the Dietenhofer home in Los Olivos, so the family felt it was appropriate to name the brewery after this beloved local landmark. Jim passed away in 2019, but Jaime and the rest of the family still run the brewery.

The brewery boasts four locations (including the Los Olivos taproom, which opened in 2014) and over 200 awards, including eight World Beer Cup awards and thirty-one Great American Beer Fest (GABF) medals. The Davy Brown Ale is named after the late 1800s pioneer and the eponymous trail near Fig Mountain. This dark, malty brew has won two GABF gold medals and is Jim's wife Judie's favorite beer. When-ever the team brews it, they put aside a case for Judie and call it the "Judie Tax."

LAND MANAGER

Los Padres National Forest
Santa Lucia District
1616 No. Carlotti Drive
Santa Maria, CA 93454
(805) 623-0328
www.fs.usda.gov/detail/lpnf/recreation/?cid=stelprdb5307963
Map: https://www.fs.usda.gov/Internet/FSE_DOCUMENTS/
fsm9_033964.pdf

BREWERY/RESTAURANT

Figueroa Mountain Brewing Co. Los Olivos
2363 Alamo Pintado Ave
Los Olivos, CA 93441
(805) 697-7601
www.figmtnbrew.com

Distance from trailhead: 13.2 miles

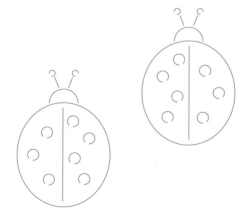

GOLETA MONARCH BUTTERFLY GROVE

SEE THOUSANDS OF MONARCH BUTTERFLIES AND CATCH AN OCEAN VIEW

GOLETA

▷⋯ STARTING POINT	⋯✕ DESTINATION
OCEAN WALK LANE	**MONARCH BUTTERFLY GROVE**
🍺 BREWERY	🗺 HIKE TYPE
DRAUGHTSMEN ALEWORKS	**EASY** 🚶
🐾 DOG FRIENDLY	📅 SEASON
YES (LEASH REQUIRED)	**OCTOBER–FEBRUARY**
$ FEES	🕐 DURATION
NONE	**1 HOUR 20 MIN.**
⛰ MAP REFERENCE	↦ LENGTH
GOLETA BUTTERFLY GROVE	**3.2 MILES** (LOLLIPOP LOOP)
🔍 HIGHLIGHTS	〰 ELEVATION GAIN
MONARCH BUTTERFLIES, OCEAN VIEWS	**174 FEET**

CEREAL KILLER
PALE ALE

5.4% ALCOHOL CONTENT

 DARK GOLDEN

 TANGERINE, GUAVA

 TROPICAL FRUIT, LIGHT

BITTERNESS

SWEETNESS

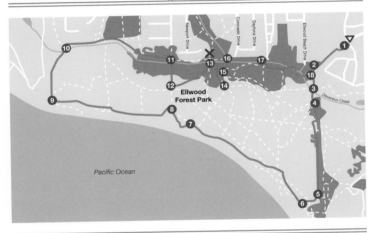

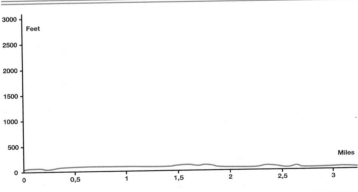

HIKE DESCRIPTION

Bring your binoculars and zoom camera lens on this three-mile stroll to see thousands of monarch butterflies and stunning ocean views. Then kick back at the welcoming Draughtsmen Aleworks and soak in the local community.

Ellwood Mesa Open Space is home to native grasslands, coastal bluffs, raptor sites, and, most notably, monarch butterfly roosting sites. From October to February, monarch butterflies overwinter all along the California coast after migrating thousands of miles from as far north as Canada. Monarch butterflies are unique because their migrations take place over multiple generations, yet they somehow still follow the same path. Each year, the new set of monarchs are four generations removed from last year's overwintering monarchs.

Over the past twenty years, monarch populations have seen a huge decline, but there are some hopeful signs of growth: the western monarch population went from under 2,000 in 2020–21 to over 200,000 in 2021–22. During a good year, the last mile and a half of this trail will take you through a eucalyptus forest with thousands of monarchs perched in the trees. You'll have to look closely, though—without binoculars or a high-powered zoom camera, the clusters of butterflies look like dead leaves and cobwebs hanging from the branches. If you're in a hurry, reverse the loop and do this section first so you can take your time here.

There are many variations of this loop trail that make it shorter or longer and several different parking areas to start from. For this version, you'll start in a small parking lot next to a residential development and set out on a trail marked with a Goleta Open Space interpretive display. At first, you'll be on an unremarkable dirt road, but after a right turn,

you'll quickly leave the residential area behind, taking a smaller dirt path into a eucalyptus forest. Soon you'll come out of the trees to open grasslands and follow the ocean breeze on a dirt path to the coast.

Starting around half a mile in, you'll enjoy a mile of almost constant ocean views with several beach access points. Two interpretive displays on this part of the trail provide information about the area's conservation status as a marine protected area providing essential habitats for various species of wildlife, including monarchs, whales, and the threatened western snowy plover. Finally, you'll turn away from the ocean and walk next to a golf course before heading onto another dirt path through the eucalyptus forest and into the monarch butterfly grove.

TURN-BY-TURN DIRECTIONS

1. From the parking lot, cross the street and take the dirt path next to the large Open Space interpretive display. After around 70 feet, turn left onto an unmarked dirt path lined with grass.
2. At 0.1 miles, reach a triangle intersection and take the unmarked trail to the left.
3. At 0.2 miles, after crossing a small creek with stump stepping stones, reach another triangle intersection and continue straight on the unmarked trail going towards the ocean.
4. At the fork at 0.3 miles, veer left. Then, less than 100 feet later, take the unmarked right turn at a T-junction. Follow the path around to the left and straight through another trail intersection.
5. At 0.6 miles, veer right and follow the unmarked curving dirt path to the edge of the coastal bluff.
6. At a T-junction at 0.7 miles, take a right onto an unmarked trail along the coast.
7. Continue on this clear main path until 1.2 miles, when an unmarked left turn veers off the main path through a shade covering of California bay laurel trees. Continue to an outcrop vista point with a small wooden bench. Follow the trail to curve back to the main path, passing an interpretive display, a sign for the western snowy plover habitat area, and a beach access trail.
8. When you reach the main unmarked trail again at 1.3 miles, take a left.
9. Continue straight along the coastline until you hit the golf course at 1.7 miles; then turn right, going inland on the unmarked trail and following the edge of the golf course.
10. At a triangle intersection at 1.9 miles, take the unmarked right trail.

11. At an intersection with a wide dirt path at 2.2 miles and just before a sign for Ellwood Main Monarch Butterfly Grove, turn right to head out of the forest and back towards the coast. For a slightly shorter route, you can continue straight, following signs directly to the butterfly grove.

12. At 2.3 miles, take an unmarked left and veer back towards the eucalyptus trees again. This trail will continue to curve left back down into the eucalyptus, and you can start looking for butterflies.

13. At the intersection at 2.5 miles, pass a wooden City of Goleta sign for Ellwood Main Monarch Butterfly Grove; then turn right and take another right after a few paces, following the posted butterfly signs.

14. At 2.6 miles, take two lefts switchbacking back down parallel to the path you were just on.

15. At a triangle intersection at 2.7 miles, keep right on the unmarked trail and veer left at a wide fork and head downhill. If it has recently rained, this part can be muddy or flooded.

16. At a T-junction less than 0.1 miles later, turn right and walk along a short line of bamboo.

17. At 2.8 miles, pass through two tan metal gates and turn right on the unmarked trail away from the road. Ignore all other trail spurs and continue on this flat part of the trail.

18. At 3.1 miles, reach the first triangle intersection and keep straight, rejoining the original path back to the parking lot.

FIND THE TRAILHEAD

From Santa Barbara, take 101 North for around 11 miles to Exit 108 for Glen Annie Rd. Turn left onto Glen Annie Rd. After going under the freeway, take a right on Hollister Ave. and continue straight for 0.7 miles. Turn left onto Cannon Green Dr.; after 0.5 miles, the road becomes Ocean Walk Ln. The small parking lot will be on the left around 50 feet before the first residential house.

DRAUGHTSMEN ALEWORKS

Draughtsmen Aleworks started as five friends getting together in a garage and drinking beer. The group officially opened Draughtsmen in 2015, but head brewer Reno King has been brewing for over twelve years. The brewery has become a thriving community hub with groups that regularly meet to play pool, relax after a bike ride, do yoga, or play bingo. Along with serving a diverse lineup of beers, wine, cider, and hop tea, the brewery gives back to the community through a monthly "good karma" beer: for every good karma pint sold, they give one dollar to a designated local not-for-profit. The Cereal Killer is a 99% gluten-reduced beer. It's a pale ale made from barley, but King uses an enzyme that removes the gluten.

LAND MANAGER

Ellwood Mesa Open Space
130 Cremona Drive
Suite B, Goleta, CA 93117
(805) 961-7500
www.cityofgoleta.org/play/ellwood-mesa-and-monarch-butterfly-habitat
Map: www.cityofgoleta.org/home/showpublisheddocument/
21675/636858225512230000

BREWERY/RESTAURANT

Draughtsmen Aleworks
53 Santa Felicia Dr
Goleta, CA 93117
(805) 387-2577
www.draughtsmenaleworks.com/

Distance from trailhead: 0.9 miles

MONTECITO PEAK

A CHALLENGING HIKE WITH ENDLESS OCEAN VIEWS OVER SANTA BARBARA

MONTECITO

▷⋯ STARTING POINT	⋯✕ DESTINATION
COLD SPRING TRAILHEAD	**MONTECITO PEAK**
🍺 BREWERY	🎴 HIKE TYPE
THIRD WINDOW BREWING COMPANY	**STRENUOUS**
🐾 DOG FRIENDLY	📅 SEASON
YES (LEASH REQUIRED)	**YEAR-ROUND**
$ FEES	🕐 DURATION
NONE	**3 HOURS 20 MIN.**
⛰ MAP REFERENCE	↦ LENGTH
POSTED AT TRAILHEAD	**6.8 MILES** (LOLLIPOP LOOP)
🔎 HIGHLIGHTS	〰 ELEVATION GAIN
MOUNTAIN OVERLOOKS, WATERFALLS, RIVERS	**2,474 FT**

5.4 %
ALCOHOL CONTENT

THE DARK LAGER

 COFFEE

 COFFEE, CHOCOLATE

 BROWN SUGAR, DARK CHOCOLATE

BITTERNESS

SWEETNESS

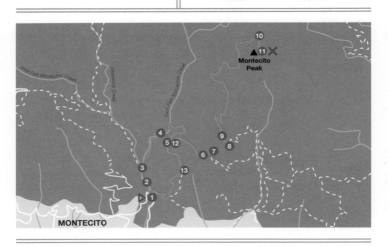

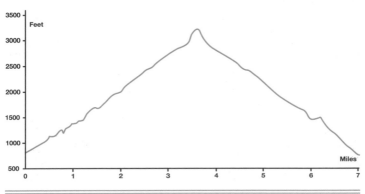

HIKE DESCRIPTION

 This difficult hike will get your blood flowing while the almost nonstop views of the ocean and Santa Barbara will keep you motivated to reach the top. Mind your step on the steep hike down and then indulge with an award-winning dark lager at Third Window Brewing.

While many of the mountains and hikes in Los Padres National Forest above Santa Barbara offer expansive views of the rolling mountains and the occasional ocean vista point, the Cold Spring Trail up to Montecito Peak provides almost constant views of the ocean, Santa Barbara, and the surrounding hills. Aside from a few flatter sections, the trail is steep but manageable the entire way to the peak, but it does have some technical rocky passages.

One of the nice things about this mountain range is that nearly all the trails running up and down these canyons connect in one way or another, so you can go for as long as you'd like. Our lollipop loop offers plenty of challenges for even experienced hikers, but if you want to add more, there are various trail spurs and additional sections you could tack on. There are also several places you can make the route shorter for a less challenging but still rewarding day.

For the first mile of the trail, you'll hike along Montecito Creek. Around a quarter mile into the hike, you'll reach the signposted Cold Spring, where East Fork Montecito Creek converges with West Fork Montecito Creek. If the creek is flowing, you'll see several small waterfalls around Cold Spring and a larger, approximately 10-foot waterfall around a half mile further down the trail. After the first mile, you'll head away from the creek and get into some steeper, forested terrain that quickly becomes chaparral. The next two miles are steep and challenging, on a red rocky singletrack path. At around 1.7 miles, you'll see a small, unmarked dirt path veering to the right into a canyon—this leads to hot springs pools where you can take a dip.

The last 0.2 miles to the peak get especially steep and technical, so choose your steps carefully. Trekking poles can be a big help on this section. At the top, look for a rock with a metal pole in it and two metal boxes—these have a series of logbooks of people summiting over the years. You can add your name and note to the books and read other people's reports (if you find the blue 2023 logbook, you may even find my note from June 2023!).

Over recent years, this area has taken a beating from heavy rainstorms. The park services have been trying to keep up with trail maintenance, adding new trail markers and keeping the trails clean, but keep in mind that the trail may be slightly altered due to erosion, mudslides, and downed trees.

TURN-BY-TURN DIRECTIONS

1. Start on the marked "East Fork Cold Spring Trail" just off the road next to a large bulletin board with a map.
2. At 0.1 miles, continue straight on the main trail, ignoring a small trail on the left.
3. At 0.2 miles, reach the signposted Cold Spring; continue to the right on the East Fork Trail.
4. At 0.6 miles, reach a waterfall. Cross the creek just in front of the waterfall and continue on the clear trail.
5. Ignore any smaller trail spurs and stay on the main track until you reach an intersection at 1.2 miles, where you'll take a sharp left following arrows on a posted wooden sign for the East Fork trail.
6. At 1.5 miles, keep left on the East Fork Trail in the direction of the power lines.
7. At 1.6 miles, the Edison access dirt road will go out right. Skip this road and continue on the unmarked trail on the left.
8. At 1.7 miles, you'll see another small dirt path on your right starting to switchback into the canyon below. This leads to the hot springs pools, a fun optional addition. Our hike skips this path and continues to the left.
9. At an unmarked T-junction at 1.8 miles, turn right and head uphill.
10. Ignore all other trail spurs and keep on the clear main path until 3.3 miles, where you'll see a steep and narrow unmarked trail on the right. The next 0.1 miles is the most technical part of the hike, with big steps and loose rock and dirt.
11. When you reach a group of large boulders at 3.6 miles, take a sharp right uphill; the summit will be around 150 feet ahead.
12. Return the way you came until the intersection at 5.9 miles, where you'll find the marked wooden signpost mentioned in Step 5. Follow the Ridge Trail, opposite to the way you came.
13. At 6.2 miles, veer right on the Ridge Trail. Continue on this main path until you reach the trailhead.

FIND THE TRAILHEAD

From Santa Barbara, head northeast on E Cota St. for around 1.3 miles. Turn right onto Alameda Padre Serra and continue for 0.9 miles to Barker Pass Rd. After around 0.8 miles, turn right on Sycamore Canyon Rd; then take a left onto Cold Spring Rd. Stay on Cold Spring Rd for 1.1 miles and then turn right on E Mountain Dr. The trailhead will be on your left after 0.3 miles, just after crossing a bridge over the river.

THIRD WINDOW BREWING

Owner and head brewer Kristopher Parker started homebrewing in 2006, but his family has been in the wine business all his life. In 2014, Parker's friend and owner of The Bruery, Patrick Rue, gave Parker his old Santa Barbara brewhouse which, in 2016, became Third Window Brewing Co. The brewery specializes in farmhouse beers with yearly vintages and has started growing its own barley and wheat. The Dark Lager won the 2021 Great American Beer Festival gold medal for international dark lager. It has rich, complex flavors but is still light enough to be refreshing after a tough hike.

LAND MANAGER

Los Padres National Forest
3505 Paradise Rd.
Santa Barbara, CA 93105
(805) 967-3481
www.fs.usda.gov/lpnf
Map: www.fs.usda.gov/recmain/lpnf/recreation

BREWERY/RESTAURANT

Third Window Brewing Company
406 E Haley St #3
Santa Barbara, CA 93101
(805) 979-5090
www.thirdwindowbrewing.com/

Distance from trailhead: 4.3 miles

VENTURA

SANTA PAULA CANYON AND PUNCH BOWLS

JOURNEY TO A SUBLIME WATERFALL AND SWIMMING HOLE

SANTA PAULA

▷··· STARTING POINT	···✕ DESTINATION
SANTA PAULA CANYON TRAILHEAD	FIRST PUNCH BOWL FALLS
🍺 BREWERY	🈺 HIKE TYPE
OJAI VALLEY BREWERY	MODERATE 🚶
🐾 DOG FRIENDLY	📅 SEASON
YES (LEASH REQUIRED)	YEAR-ROUND
$ FEES	🕐 DURATION
NO	4 HOURS 45 MIN.
⛰ MAP REFERENCE	↦ LENGTH
HIKE LOS PADRES	8.2 MILES (ROUND TRIP)
🔍 HIGHLIGHTS	〰 ELEVATION GAIN
WATERFALLS, CREEK WALKING	1,056 FEET

 6.0% ALCOHOL CONTENT

CHAPARRAL HERB ALE

 GOLD

 SAGE, FLORAL

 HERBAL, CRISP

BITTERNESS SWEETNESS

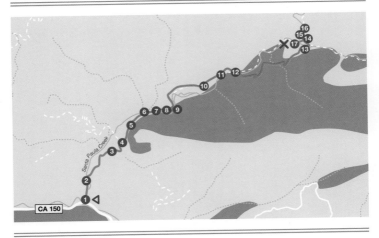

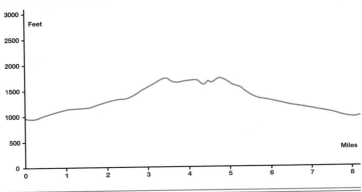

HIKE DESCRIPTION

Hike along a creek to the first of a series of falls feeding into emerald pools perfect for a refreshing swim. Afterwards, get a taste of the landscape you've just been hiking in with Ojai Valley Brewery's Chaparral, which is brewed with local sage.

Punchbowl waterfalls flow forcefully through a single narrow channel into a circular pool. The Santa Paula Punch Bowls (sometimes spelled punchbowls) consist of one such falls and additional swimming holes.

Starting from the parking area, this trail gets right into the fun part, leading down to the river and two creek crossings. With some tactical log walking and rock jumping, you might be able to keep your feet dry, but there are many more crossings to come that will likely get them wet. Wear quick-drying or well-draining shoes with good grips to make these crossings easier and more comfortable. The trail can be hard to see along the creek because storms regularly change the landscape, but there are black diamonds spray-painted on rocks to keep you from getting lost.

The first mile and a half is on private property; you'll pass a small house, an avocado farm, and two oil wells. Once you pass these landmarks and head into the national forest, you'll return to the creek and navigate several more creek crossings while going back and forth between the rocky bed and a dirt trail just above the creek.

Around two-and-a-half miles into the hike, you'll diverge from the creek and head up a dirt trail that climbs up along the canyon through chaparral. After a little under a mile of uphill hiking, the trail flattens out and you'll reach a clearing surrounded by pine and oak trees with a small firepit in the middle; this is the Big Cone campsite.

After passing the campsite, you'll meet back up with the creek and cross a tiered set of small falls. Soon you'll reach the turn for the first and main punch bowl. You'll skip this turn for now and continue straight to climb above the falls for an aerial view of the creek and canyon. A little further on, you'll also get a view of the narrow slot canyon of light gray rock that the river carves its way through. Then you'll turn around and head back to the first falls, where you can take in the 25-foot waterfall and the beautiful swimming hole. However, if you want to continue instead of turning around, in about a mile you'll come upon the second and third punch bowls—two more swimming holes with places for rock jumping and a natural waterslide (depending on water levels).

TURN-BY-TURN DIRECTIONS

1. From the parking lot, head through the gate and follow the main trail leading to the river and the first river crossing. Follow the black diamonds spray-painted on rocks to navigate along the rocky creek.

2. At 0.2 miles, cross the river again; then follow the trail away from the creek through a chaparral landscape.

3. At 0.7 miles, pass a small house on the left and some orange trees on the right. Rounding a corner, you'll see an oil well on the right. Keep left, following the arrow indicating trail access, and pass under the entrance sign for Rancho Recuerdo.

4. At 0.8 miles, keep right in the direction indicated by a large sign with an arrow and the word "Trail." Pass through an avocado orchard on a wide paved road.

5. At 1.1 miles, reach a fenced-off oil well and continue to the left on the signposted trail leading along the fence.

6. At 1.2 miles, hike along the rocky creek following the black diamonds. Over the next 500 feet, you'll want to cross the creek to end up on the left side. This section is regularly changing due to water levels and flooding, so use your best judgment about where to cross.

7. At 1.3 miles, follow a small path on the left marked with black diamonds leading away from the creek through a stand of trees.

8. At 1.5 miles, come to a small clearing and keep right as indicated by the arrow for "Hiking trail."

9. At 1.6 miles, cross the creek two more times, following the black diamonds. Continue through a dry creek bed marked with black diamonds.

10. At 2.1 miles, follow the black diamonds out of the dry creek bed to the left and up a rocky trail. At a T-junction 100 feet ahead, keep right.

11. At 2.4 miles, return to the creek and cross it.

12. At 2.5 miles, cross the creek again and then follow the black diamonds to the right of the creek heading uphill on a rocky trail.

13. At 3.6 miles, reach the creek at a small, tiered falls. Cross the creek and climb a rocky section up to a trail marker. Keep left on the Last Chance Trail.

14. At 3.8 miles, pass a small, unmarked trail on the left and continue straight. This is the trail to the falls you'll return to.

15. At 3.9 miles, reach a canyon overlook view; continue on the trail.

16. At 4.0 miles, reach the creek above the falls and see the water cascading over gray rock and carving its way through a slot canyon down to the falls. From here, turn around and return to the unmarked turn at Step 14.

17. At 4.3 miles, reach the turn you passed in Step 14 and turn right, going down the hill. This leads to the falls and first punch bowl. Return to the trailhead the way you came.

FIND THE TRAILHEAD

From Ventura, take US-101 S towards Los Angeles. After 3.4 miles, keep right for CA-126 E towards Santa Clarita. After 12.3 miles, take the exit for 10th St./CA-150 and Santa Paula. At the end of the off-ramp, turn left onto 10th St./CA-150. Proceed for 5.9 miles until you see a small dirt pull-off on the right 400 feet past the right turn for Thomas Aquinas College. This lot is often full, but you can find additional parking further along the road or on the left just before Thomas Aquinas College.

OJAI VALLEY BREWERY

A small local brewhouse, Ojai Valley Brewery prides itself on offering up the unique taste of the surrounding landscape by using local botanicals in its beers. Owner and brewmaster Jeremy Haffner previously owned a restaurant in town with his wife Elizabeth Haffner (she's now COO of the brewery and runs her own consulting business for novice restaurateurs). When Jeremy founded the brewery in 2016, he teamed up with current head brewer Griffin Davis. The team started brewing in 2017, and when the Haffners sold their restaurant in 2021, the brewery opened the current taproom and beer garden.

The Chaparral amber ale was one of the first beers the brewery made and has black sage, white sage, and purple sage infused in the brew. Davis originally foraged the wild sage for the beer while on local hikes. Now, the team grows most of the sage on the Haffner's property.

LAND MANAGER

Los Padres National Forest
Ojai Ranger District
1190 E Ojai Ave.
Ojai, CA 93023
(805) 968-6640 or (805) 724-0079
www.fs.usda.gov/recarea/lpnf/recreation/hiking/recarea/
?recid=11020&actid=51
Map: www.hikelospadres.com/santa-paula-canyon-trail.html

BREWERY/RESTAURANT

Ojai Valley Brewery
307 Bryant St.
Ojai, CA 93023
www.ojaivalleybrewery.com/

Distance from trailhead: 10.5 miles

ANACAPA INSPIRATION POINT

EXPLORE THE SECOND-SMALLEST ISLAND IN CHANNEL ISLANDS NATIONAL PARK

VENTURA

▷··· STARTING POINT	···✗ DESTINATION
ISLAND PACKERS CRUISES HARBOR	**INSPIRATION POINT**
🍺 BREWERY	HIKE TYPE
TOPA TOPA BREWING COMPANY	**EASY**
🐾 DOG FRIENDLY	📅 SEASON
NO	**YEAR-ROUND**
$ FEES	🕐 DURATION
YES (FERRY TRANSPORT)	**1 HOUR 30 MIN.**
⌖ MAP REFERENCE	↦ LENGTH
ANACAPA ISLAND HIKING MAP	**2.7 MILES** (LOOP)
🔍 HIGHLIGHTS	〰 °ELEVATION GAIN
ISLAND LOOKOUTS, WHALE WATCHING	**318 FEET**

5.5%
ALCOHOL CONTENT

CALIFORNIA NITRO PUB ALE

FOAMY,
GOLDEN

BREADY,
ORANGE

MALTY,
BREAD

BITTERNESS

SWEETNESS

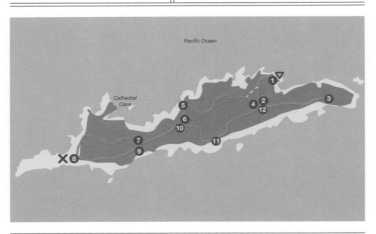

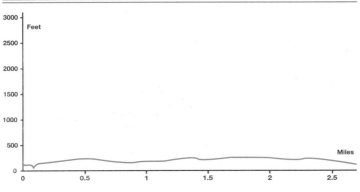

HIKE DESCRIPTION

Enjoy a magical hour-long ferry ride and then hike around the entire East Anacapa Island, with breathtaking views from every angle. Once you return to Ventura harbor, head to Topa Topa Brewing Company's headquarters for a fresh and local nitro pour in the beer garden.

While Anacapa is only 13 miles from Ventura and the mainland, the island feels like its own world—and in a way, it is. Because of the Channel Islands' isolation from the mainland, they have their own micro-eco-systems with unique species like the Anacapa deer mouse, which is only found on Anacapa Island (and is the only mammal on the island to boot). The islands also provide essential habitats for a wide variety of birds including California brown pelicans, western gulls, and Scripps's murrelets.

Approximately five miles long, a quarter-mile wide, and with an area of only one square mile, Anacapa is the second-smallest of the five Channel Islands (second only to Santa Barbara Island). However, the amount of accessible terrain is even smaller because Anacapa is actually made up of three islets: East, Middle, and West Anacapa Islands. The only islet visitors can hike on is East Anacapa. This short stroll will take you on a figure-eight loop covering the entire islet.

Unless you have a private boat, your adventure will begin at Ventura Harbor with Island Packers Cruises—book well in advance because these sell out! The ferry ride is about an hour long. If you're lucky, you may see wildlife such as whales, dolphins, orcas, sea lions, and pelicans. The hiking begins when the boat docks at Landing Cove, a small inlet sheltered by towering volcanic sea cliffs. To get to land, you'll climb a short steel ladder and then a long series of stairs—157 steps, to be exact. Once you've made this climb, the rest of the hike is a relaxing stroll on relatively flat trails.

The views you'll see on the island depend on the season and weather. Summer can be rather desolate and hot because the island has no source of fresh water and virtually no shade. However, summer is the best time to see blue and humpback whales and cute western gull hatchlings. Fall is the best time for water activities like snorkeling, diving, and kayaking, with warmer water and high underwater visibility. On a sunny spring day, the island flaunts vibrant greens, yellows, pinks, purples, and whites from various wildflowers, other ground cover, and the hundreds of western gulls wandering about.

You'll begin the walk passing a small visitor center (well worth a peek) and head slightly uphill to the far eastern point of the island for an up-close view of the picturesque lighthouse, which entered service in 1932 and was the last permanent lighthouse built on the West Coast.

From the lighthouse, you'll head back past the visitor center and hike along the north side of the island, where you'll come upon Cathedral Cove—a gorgeous blue inlet. Then you're off to the far western bit of land, Inspiration Point. Here, you'll enjoy one of the iconic Channel Island views of the razor ridgeline pointing out to the other islands beyond. On the second half of the loop, be sure to pause at Pinniped Point and look for sea lions lounging in the water or on the rocky outcrops below.

TURN-BY-TURN DIRECTIONS

1. After disembarking from the boat and climbing the stairs to Landing Cove, head uphill along the wide dirt road.
2. At 0.2 miles, come to an intersection of four trails and a collection of single-story buildings including the ranger station, visitor center, and bathrooms. Pass the buildings and head left towards the lighthouse.
3. At 0.5 miles, reach the lighthouse. Turn around and retrace your steps back to the visitor center.
4. At 0.8 miles, reach the visitor center again and follow the trail in front of the visitor center for Cathedral Cove and Inspiration point.
5. At 1.1 miles, reach Cathedral Cove on the right. After enjoying the view, continue following the main trail for Campground and Inspiration Point.
6. At 1.2 miles, keep right for Inspiration Point.
7. At 1.4 miles, turn right for Inspiration Point.
8. At 1.7 miles, reach Inspiration Point. This is a good place for a snack or photos. From here, continue along the wide trail curving around the island.
9. At 2.0 miles, continue straight, closing the Inspiration Point mini-loop.
10. At 2.1 miles, veer right for Campground and Pinniped Point.
11. At 2.3 miles, reach Pinniped Point and look for sea lions in the water below.
12. At 2.5 miles, pass the visitor center a final time and continue straight to return to Landing Cove.

FIND THE TRAILHEAD

From downtown Ventura, head south on S California St. for around 0.2 miles until the road ends at a T-junction with E Harbor Blvd. Turn left onto E Harbor Blvd. After 3.4 miles, turn right onto Spinnaker Dr. After 1.0 miles, the parking lot for Island Packers will be on the right.

TOPA TOPA BREWING COMPANY

Topa Topa Brewing Company opened its first fifteen-barrel brewhouse in June 2015 in an old printing press in downtown Ventura, just two blocks from Patagonia. In two years, Topa Topa outgrew the initial facility and expanded to its new headquarters on Colt St., which features a luxurious outdoor space, rotating food trucks, and eighteen different taps to choose from. The original location in downtown Ventura is still alive and well, along with three other locations in Santa Barbara, Ojai, and Camarillo.

Co-founder and brewmaster Casey Harris began his career at Stone Brewing Company but had fallen in love with beer well before then while homebrewing in college; he had planned to go to law school but instead decided to pursue his passion for great beer. Together with co-owner Jack Dyer, he now creates award-winning brews and supports community-based initiatives and environmental causes through 1% for the Planet. The California Nitro Pub Ale is only available in Topa Topa's taprooms. The brewers use 100% California-grown ingredients to create a rich, bready, British pub ale–style brew.

LAND MANAGER

Channel Islands National Park
1901 Spinnaker Drive
Ventura, CA 93001
(805) 658-5730
www.nps.gov/chis/index.htm
Map: www.nps.gov/chis/planyourvisit/upload/ai-hiking-2022-ADA.pdf

BREWERY/RESTAURANT

Topa Topa Brewing Company
4880 Colt St,
Ventura, CA 93003
(805) 535-4366
www.topatopa.beer/

Distance from trailhead: 3.9 miles

PARADISE FALLS

SHORT, FAMILY-FRIENDLY WATERFALL EXCURSION

THOUSAND OAKS

▷⋯ STARTING POINT	⋯✗ DESTINATION
WILDWOOD REGIONAL PARK TRAILHEAD	**PARADISE FALLS**
🍺 BREWERY	🀫 HIKE TYPE
NAUGHTY PINE BREWING COMPANY	**EASY**
🐾 DOG FRIENDLY	📅 SEASON
YES (LEASH REQUIRED)	**YEAR-ROUND**
$ FEES	🕐 DURATION
NO	**1 HOUR 20 MIN.**
⌂ MAP REFERENCE	↦ LENGTH
POSTED AT TRAILHEAD	**2.4 MILES** (LOOP)
🔎 HIGHLIGHTS	〰 ELEVATION GAIN
WATERFALL, CAVE, WOMAN-OWNED BREWERY	**381 FEET**

4.8 %
ALCOHOL
CONTENT

STURDY-B PILSNER

 PALE STRAW

 GRAINY, BREADY

 GRAHAM CRACKER, LIGHT

BITTERNESS   SWEETNESS

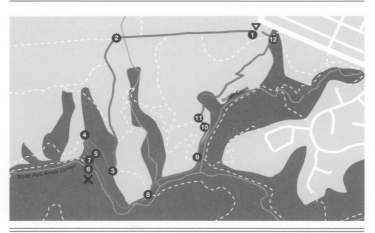

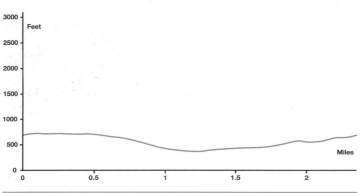

HIKE DESCRIPTION

Hike to this 40-foot waterfall and explore the ecologically diverse landscape of Wildwood Regional Park. Posthike, head over to Naughty Pine Brewing Company for one of brewer and owner Brittany Brouhard's refreshing and unique beers.

Wildwood Regional Park consists of 1,745 acres of land with a rich history and a wide variety of different plants and animals. As you set off on the hike, you'll follow a wide dirt path through hilly grasslands with views of the rocky Mount Clef Ridge rising up on the right. This volcanic ridge was formed by lava eruptions thirty million years ago. When you turn off the Mesa Trail, you'll start a mild descent along another wide dirt trail leading directly to the Wildwood "Teepee"—an interesting structure that provides shade and a seating area, but bears little resemblance to an actual Native American teepee. In fact, the Native Americans of this area—the Chumash people—wouldn't have used teepees at all; they used a dome structure called an 'ap, traditionally made from willow poles and the native plant

tule. To learn more about the Chumash people, visit the Chumash Indian Museum in nearby Oakbrook Regional Park, which is also the site of a former Chumash village called Sapwi (House of Deer).

From the Teepee, you'll head down a wide trail with views of the rolling hillside. The trail narrows and leads into more oak trees and riparian habitat as you come to the 40-foot waterfall and the rocky pool at its base. Both natural and urban runoff feed the falls, meaning the water isn't safe to swim in, but it is a cool (both in terms of temperature and views) spot for lunch or a snack.

From the falls, you'll climb back up a set of stairs and continue on a path following the river above the waterfall. This part of the trail is shaded by oaks, willows, and cottonwoods. On your way uphill from the creek, you'll come upon Little Cave (recently renamed from Indian Cave), an eroded bit of sandstone. Scrambling through the cave (or walking around it), you'll reach a small trail leading into a very different landscape.

The final stretch of the hike passes through a desertlike coastal sage scrub habitat where you'll see prickly pear cactus and the radiant yellow flowers of California brittlebush.

TURN-BY-TURN DIRECTIONS

1. From the parking lot, head uphill on the Mesa Trail, passing the information bulletin. Continue straight for Paradise Falls, ignoring various trail diversions on either side.
2. At 0.4 miles, veer left on the Teepee and Paradise Falls Trail. Continue straight, ignoring all other trails to the left and right.
3. At 0.8 miles, reach Wildwood Teepee. At the intersection here, turn right on the Paradise Falls Trail.
4. At 0.9 miles, take a sharp left to remain on the Paradise Falls Trail.
5. At the intersection at 1.0 miles, take a sharp right and head downhill on switchbacks. After around 100 feet, turn left on the Paradise Falls Trail.
6. After a set of stairs, reach Paradise Falls at 1.1 miles. For the best view of the falls, cross the creek with some strategic rock and log jumping. Head back up the stairs you came down on.
7. At 1.3 miles, at the intersection mentioned in step 5, take the unmarked Wildwood Canyon Trail to the right following a chain-link fence—opposite the trail you approached on.
8. At 1.5 miles, continue straight on the Wildwood Canyon Trail in the direction of the Nature Center.
9. At 1.7 miles, reach an intersection with a bridge crossing the creek on the right. Keep left to stay on the left side of the creek and then head slightly right towards Indian/Little Cave.
10. At 1.8 miles, reach Indian/Little Cave. You can climb into and through the cave to reach a small overgrown trail that continues uphill. If you don't feel comfortable scrambling into the cave, you can follow a vague trail around the cave to reach the top of the cave.
11. At 1.9 miles, emerge onto a more defined trail and turn right on it.
12. At 2.3 miles, turn left and head up the staircase leading to the parking lot.

FIND THE TRAILHEAD

From Thousand Oaks, take US-101 N. After 3.2 miles, take Exit 45 for Lynn Rd. Turn right onto Lynn Rd. and proceed for 2.5 miles. At W Avenida De Los Arboles, turn left. After 0.9 miles, just before the road turns right and becomes Big Sky Dr., the large dirt trailhead parking lot will be on the left.

NAUGHTY PINE BREWING COMPANY

Owner and head brewer Brittany Brouhard (yes, that is her real name and yes, it's pronounced similarly to "brew hard") developed an interest in brewing when she bought her future husband a homebrewing kit one Christmas while in college. In 2013, the couple got their feet wet in the industry, opening a brewery in Maui together with two other couples. Brittany then became the lead brewer at Enegren Brewing Company, where she practiced large-scale brewing for almost five years. Finally, she decided it was time to branch out and start her own brewery with her family.

The 1920s speakeasy aesthetic of the Naughty Pine Brewing taproom, based on the show Peaky Blinders, is all Brittany's doing. The brewery hosts live music almost every night of the week and puts on emo night events every other month with multiple bands, food vendors, and dark, moody decorations and lighting. Brittany prides herself on using style-specific yeast strains for each beer she crafts in her seven-barrel brew system. The diverse lineup of true-to-style beers includes the brewery's flagship Pilsner—her favorite style of beer. The Pilsner is light and crushable, perfect for after a hike on a hot day.

LAND MANAGER

Conejo Open Space Conservation Agency
403 W. Hillcrest Drive
Thousand Oaks, CA 91360
(805) 381-2741
www.conejo-openspace.org/openspace/wildwood-park/
Map: www.conejo-openspace.org/wp-content/uploads/2022/05/
Wildwood_TrailMap_2pg_20220512.pdf

BREWERY/RESTAURANT

Naughty Pine Brewing Co.
766 Lakefield Dr., Ste A
Westlake Village, CA 91361
(805) 906-2140
www.naughtypinebrewingco.com/

Distance from trailhead: 7.8 miles

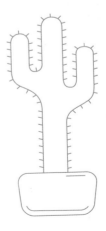

LOS ANGELES

CAVE OF MUNITS

CLIMB INTO A CATHEDRAL-LIKE CAVE

WEST HILLS

▷⋯ STARTING POINT	⋯✗ DESTINATION
EL ESCORPION CANYON PARK	**CAVE OF MUNITS**
🍺 BREWERY	🈳 HIKE TYPE
TAVERN TOMOKO AND LADYFACE BREWERY	**STRENUOUS**
🐾 DOG FRIENDLY	📅 SEASON
YES (LEASH REQUIRED)	**YEAR-ROUND**
$ FEES	🕐 DURATION
NO	**2 HOURS**
⛺ MAP REFERENCE	↦ LENGTH
UPPER LAS VIRGENES CANYON OPEN SPACE PRESERVE	**2.7 MILES** (LOOP)
🔍 HIGHLIGHTS	〜 ELEVATION GAIN
ROCK SCRAMBLING, PEAK VIEWS	**774 FEET**

BLIND AMBITION BELGIAN DARK ALE

DARK CARAMEL

CARAMEL, SCOTCH

MALTY, CARAMEL

BITTERNESS

SWEETNESS

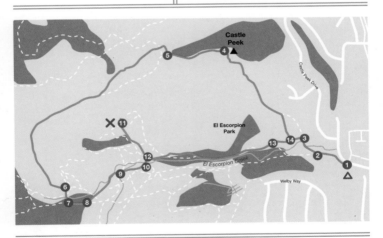

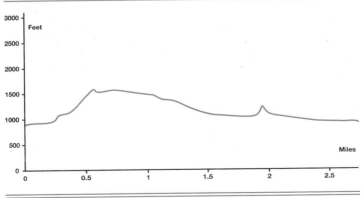

HIKE DESCRIPTION

Enjoy sweeping views from Castle Peak and scramble into a large cave with high ceilings and a cathedral-like atmosphere. After this ambitious outing, head to Tavern Tomoko and Ladyface Brewery for a pint of Blind Ambition—an award-winning Belgian-style amber ale.

This hike begins with the hardest part: the climb up to Castle Peak from El Escorpion Canyon Park. The surrounding area was previously part of the 1,110-acre Rancho El Escorpion, one of very few ranchos granted to native people in 1845 and El Escorpión Canyon Park's namesake. After a flat 0.2 miles on a dirt path leading away from the road, you'll round a corner and see your destination looming ahead. Castle Peak's name is a corruption of the Chumash name, Kas'elew (the tongue). This peak was an important ceremonial site for the Chumash people.

The hike up to Castle Peak is steep, climbing approximately 550 feet in 0.4 miles with a 40 percent gradient at times. It takes some mild scrambling at the end to reach the rocky summit, but the views of the surrounding hills and the town below offer a satisfying reward.

The trail continues along the ridge becoming much less defined, particularly in spring when the grasses start to grow over it. The plus side of the unmarked, overgrown trail is the remote and rugged feeling you'll enjoy wading through head-high wild mustard flowers.

Approaching the end of the descent, look for bright orange silly string–like vines covering plants such as California sagebrush and white sage. This bright orange "string" is an annual, native parasitic plant called

California Dodder that comes out in spring and summer. California Dodder taps into its host's stem and communicates with it via microRNA to keep its defense system quiet while it saps the nutrients it needs. (The host usually survives the onslaught.)

As the slope flattens, you'll emerge on a wide dirt trail and start turning back in the direction of the trailhead. You'll diverge onto a small, less defined trail leading under several oak trees. From here, you'll be able to spot the rock on the hillside and the long slit opening for the Cave of Munits. You can admire this sedimentary rock cave from the base, but if you're up for some moderate scrambling, climbing inside the cave is a truly unique experience. It's around 15–20 feet wide but goes at least 200 feet into the rock while its walls shoot up approximately 100 feet. Holes in the top allow rays of natural light to beam down into it. A Chumash myth called the khra'wiyawi' (the chief of Tujunga) describes how a shaman named Munits captured the son of the chief and killed him at the cave; in turn, Munits was killed on Castle Peak.

Some people scramble up the cave and out a hole in the top to climb up to Castle Peak; on our route, however, you'll emerge from the cave the way you entered. From here, you'll close the loop hiking along a well-established dirt trail.

TURN-BY-TURN DIRECTIONS

1. From the trailhead off Sunset Ridge Ct., follow the unmarked dirt path; this runs parallel to the road and then veers off to the left.
2. At 0.1 miles, keep right on the unmarked trail through oak trees, heading up towards a rocky peak.
3. At 0.2 miles, after crossing a (usually dry) creek bed, turn left on an unmarked trail; proceed for around 200 feet and turn right onto a small, steep, unmarked trail heading towards the rocky peak above.
4. At 0.5 miles, reach Castle Peak. Scramble to the top of the rocks or follow a small trail on the left going around the summit.
5. At 0.7 miles, reach an unmarked fork and continue straight on a small overgrown trail. Around 100 feet down the trail, veer left on another overgrown and easy-to-miss trail heading down the hillside.
6. At 1.4 miles, keep right on the unmarked trail.
7. At 1.5 miles, reach a T-junction with a wider, more established path and turn left.
8. At 1.6 miles, veer to the left off the main trail onto a small, unmarked trail in the direction of Castle Peak and the ridge that you just hiked.
9. At 1.7 miles, continue straight on an unmarked trail, ignoring a trail on the left and passing under a large oak tree.
10. At 1.8 miles, reach a T-junction with a wider unmarked path and turn left. Less than 50 feet ahead, keep left, heading uphill towards the rocky outcrops where the Cave of Munits is hidden. This begins a small detour off the main loop.
11. At 1.9 miles, reach the Cave of Munits. You can admire it from outside or scramble into the cave. Then return the way you came back towards the main loop.
12. At 2.1 miles, reach the intersection with the main loop again and head to the left on an unmarked but clear dirt trail (opposite from the way you came at Step 10). Continue straight, ignoring any smaller offshoot trails.
13. At 2.5 miles, reach an unmarked fork and keep left.
14. At 3.0 miles, reach the start of the lollipop loop and turn right to head back towards the trailhead.

FIND THE TRAILHEAD

From Los Angeles, take US-101 N for approximately 26 miles until Exit 29 for Mulholland Dr. and Valley Center Blvd. From the freeway exit, turn right onto Valley Center Blvd. and proceed for 2.9 miles. At Vanowen St., turn left; the trailhead, marked with a sign for El Escorpion Canyon Park, will be on the left in 0.1 miles.

TAVERN TOMOKO AND LADYFACE BREWERY

After working in the corporate sector for twenty years, Pete Lee decided it was time to pursue his dream: to own a brewery and a restaurant. So, when Ladyface Brewery went up for sale in 2019, he jumped at the opportunity. Named after Ladyface Mountain—the mountain you look out to from the patio—Ladyface Brewery opened in 2009, but Lee rebranded in March 2020 to include Tavern Tomoko (Lee's wife's middle name is Tomoko and means "friendly girl" in Japanese). Lee offers up American pub-style foods and contemporary Japanese tapas, so while you can order a classic burger, you can also get Robata skewers, pork gyoza, and other small dishes.

Award-winning master brewer Dave Griffiths stayed on through the transition—in fact, he's been at Ladyface since it opened in 2009. The brewery has historically specialized in Belgian-style beers, though it now offers a variety of different brews. Blind Ambition, one of the first beers the brewery developed, has a rich, malty, caramel flavor. This Belgian Abbey was one of the few beers the brewery had ingredients for in the early days. It turned out so well that they named it Blind Ambition and now regularly have it on tap.

LAND MANAGER

The Mountains Recreation and Conservation Authority (MRCA)
2600 Franklin Canyon Dr.
Beverly Hills, CA 90210
(323) 221-9944
www.mrca.ca.gov/parks/park-listing/upper-las-virgenes-canyon-open-space-preserve-formerly-ahmanson-ranch/
Map: www.mrca.ca.gov/wp-content/uploads/2018/02/ahmanson_map-1.pdf

BREWERY/RESTAURANT

Tavern Tomoko and Ladyface Brewery
29281 Agoura Rd.
Agoura Hills, CA 91301
(818) 477-4566
www.taverntomoko.com/ladyface-brewery

Distance from trailhead: 11.0 miles

ESCONDIDO FALLS

A POPULAR JAUNT TO A MULTI-TIERED WATERFALL

MALIBU

▷⋯ STARTING POINT	⋯✕ DESTINATION
ESCONDIDO CANYON PARKING	**ESCONDIDO FALLS**
🍺 BREWERY	🎲 HIKE TYPE
MALIBU BREWING COMPANY	**EASY** 🚶
🐾 DOG FRIENDLY	📅 SEASON
YES (LEASH REQUIRED)	**DECEMBER–JUNE**
$ FEES	🕐 DURATION
YES	**1 HOUR 40 MIN.**
⌂ MAP REFERENCE	↦ LENGTH
ESCONDIDO CANYON PARK MAP	**3.8 MILES** (ROUND TRIP)
🔍 HIGHLIGHTS	〰 ELEVATION GAIN
WATERFALL, WILDFLOWERS	**518 FEET**

HATCH GREEN CHILE LAGER

 PALE STRAW

 GREEN CHILE

 GREEN CHILE, SPICY

BITTERNESS

SWEETNESS

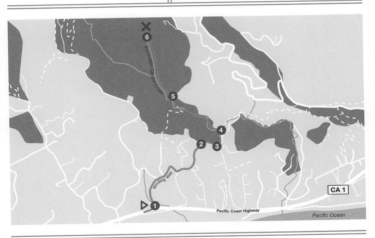

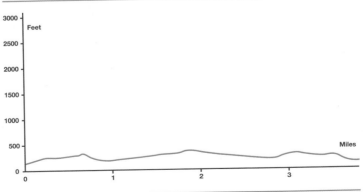

HIKE DESCRIPTION

Explore this short hike along a seasonal creek to the base of the lower tier of Escondido Falls. Then head to Malibu Brewing Company for a blast of New Mexican flavor with a spicy yet refreshing hatch green chile lager.

At 150 feet, the upper Escondido Falls is the tallest waterfall in the Santa Monica Mountains. While the upper falls is not currently open to the public, you'll enjoy a view of it plunging over a cliff edge on the way to the lower falls. The lower falls—which you'll hike to the base of—is a beautiful waterfall in its own right, cascading 50 feet into a shallow pool. While the trail is open year-round, the falls is seasonal and heavily dependent on rains and weather conditions, so it's best to visit in the winter or spring after a heavy rain.

The word Escondido is Spanish for "hidden," and that aptly describes this unique waterfall. Standing in the parking lot, you'd never guess there was a 150-foot waterfall a short 1.8 miles away. The hike, however, is far from a secret—it's heavily trafficked, especially on weekends.

From the small parking lot, you'll head up Winding Way Road, a wide paved road open only to resident traffic. The first half-mile of the hike is unconventional: it winds uphill through a neighborhood of exceptionally large houses. The road eventually leads away from the houses to give you a view of the canyon below. Soon you'll see a sign for the park and trail. You'll head down into the canyon along a narrow dirt path. As you descend, you'll face the hill on the other side of the canyon, which in the spring turns yellow with mustard flowers.

At the canyon floor, you'll reach Escondido Canyon Creek and cross it. You'll make three more creek crossings. Depending on the water level, these crossings could involve stepping across a dry creek bed, strategically traversing on logs, or wading through ankle- to shin-deep water.

From here, the trail steadily ascends along the creek under the shade of oak trees. Lining this part of the trail, you'll find the yellow, fast-growing canyon sunflower. This species is native to California and is a pioneer after wildfires. It's currently flourishing in this area thanks to the 2018 Woolsey fire, but will eventually become dominated by the slower growing chaparral shrubs.

A little after a mile, the trail comes out of the trees into a more sunny, exposed section, from which you'll be able to see the upper falls in the distance on the right. From here, the trail descends back under tree cover and leads to a clearing at the base of the lower falls.

TURN-BY-TURN DIRECTIONS

1. From the parking lot, head up Winding Way, away from the highway. Stay on the side of the paved road and do not take any side roads or driveways—these are private.
2. At 0.7 miles, reach a partial cul-de-sac and continue following the road slightly to the right and downhill with the canyon directly ahead.
3. At 0.8 miles, come to the official park trail with a sign for Edward Albert Escondido Canyon Trail and Waterfalls; turn left onto the dirt trail.
4. At 0.9 miles, cross the creek and turn left at the T-junction marked with a small wooden post labeled "Trail."
5. At an unmarked T-junction at 1.3 miles, keep left.
6. At 1.8 miles, reach the falls. Return the way you came.

FIND THE TRAILHEAD

From Los Angeles, take CA-110 S/Harbor Freeway for around one mile. Keep right and take exit 21 for I-10 W. Once you've merged onto I-10 W, proceed for 12.3 miles. This highway turns into CA-1 N (commonly called Highway 1, the Pacific Coast Highway, or the PCH). After 17.7 miles, turn right onto Winding Way and reach the trail parking, marked with a sign for the Winding Way Trail. The road will loop around to the left into the parking lot directly after you turn. You can park in this lot for a fee or park along the PCH for free except where posted.

MALIBU BREWING COMPANY

Malibu Brewing Company, Malibu's first brewery, opened in September 2022. Malibu residents Jill and Ryan Ahrens wanted to create a local spot for their community to enjoy craft beer. Besides owning the brewery, the husband-and-wife duo are co-founders of the film company Argent Pictures, which has helped produce popular films including *The Birth of a Nation*, *American Made,* and *The Social Dilemma*. Steps aways from Zuma Beach, the brewery has a laid-back and tasteful atmosphere with 24 taps and a full restaurant—the fresh-catch tacos are filled with whatever fish came off the boat that morning!

Head brewer Chas Cloud has been brewing for over a decade at various breweries throughout Southern California. Malibu Brewing Co. offers a diverse lineup of well-balanced beers, including everything from light lagers and blondes to double IPAs and barrel-aged stouts. The Hatch Green Chile Lager pays tribute to Ryan's home state, New Mexico. It has a strong green chile aroma and unique spicy flavor mixing with a light and refreshing Mexican-style lager base.

LAND MANAGER

Mountains Recreation and Conservation Authority
27200 Winding Way
Malibu, CA 90265
(323) 221-9944
www.mrca.ca.gov/parks/park-listing/escondido-canyon-park/
Map: www.mrca.ca.gov/wp-content/uploads/2018/02/escondido-1.pdf

BREWERY/RESTAURANT

Malibu Brewing Company
30745 E Pacific Coast Hwy. R4
Malibu, CA 90265
(310) 684-2408
www.brewmalibu.com/

Distance from trailhead: 4.5 miles

SKULL ROCK

DISCOVER UNIQUE ROCK FORMATIONS AND A TIERED WATERFALL

PACIFIC PALISADES

▷⋯ STARTING POINT	⋯✗ DESTINATION
TEMESCAL GATEWAY PARK	**SKULL ROCK**
🍺 BREWERY	🗺 HIKE TYPE
SANTA MONICA BREW WORKS	**MODERATE** 🚶
🐾 DOG FRIENDLY	📅 SEASON
NO	**YEAR-ROUND**
$ FEES	🕐 DURATION
YES	**2 HOURS 20 MIN.**
⛰ MAP REFERENCE	↦ LENGTH
POSTED AT TRAILHEAD	**4.5 MILES** (LOOP)
🔍 HIGHLIGHTS	〜 ELEVATION GAIN
ROCK SCRAMBLING, WILDFLOWERS, OCEAN VIEWS	**1,138 FEET**

310 STOMPED LEMONADE SHANDY

4.0% ALCOHOL CONTENT

 HAZY YELLOW

 LEMONADE

 LEMON, SOUR

BITTERNESS

SWEETNESS

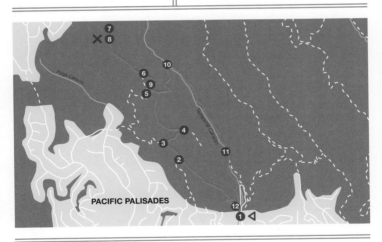

PACIFIC PALISADES

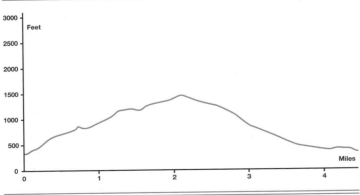

HIKE DESCRIPTION

Scramble around the unique sandstone formations at Skull Rock and enjoy sweeping views of Los Angeles and the ocean. Post-workout, head to Santa Monica Brew Works for a taste of local beach vibes with a refreshing lemonade shandy.

This hike leads through two different recreation areas: Temescal Gateway Park and Topanga State Park. Topanga State Park's 11,525 acres are mostly within the Los Angeles city limits, making it one of the world's largest wildlands within the boundaries of a major city. The name Topanga is often translated as "where the mountain meets the sea" and comes from the local Native American Tongva tribe's language.

This trail begins in Temescal Gateway Park, which serves as access to neighboring state parks and wilderness areas including Topanga State Park and Will Rogers State Historic Park. The hike begins with a steep series of switchbacks lined by yellow California Brittlebush flowers.

The California Brittlebush was used by Native Americans for various purposes: they created a glue from the stem resin and chewed the stems to relieve toothaches and gum pain.

Shortly after finishing the switchbacks, you'll reach a small lookout that offers views out to the ocean. You'll continue steadily uphill through chaparral, which offers some shade along the trail. The laurel sumac you'll encounter here is an essential native species in chaparral eco-systems, an evergreen shrub with dark red veins and stems and clusters of small aromatic white flowers. Around a mile and a half into the hike, you'll reach the turnoff for Skull Rock, which diverges off the primary loop. You'll hike along a gradually climbing ridgeline and see outcrops of Skull Rock and other sandstone boulder formations.

While there are a few different paths leading to the base of Skull Rock, the clearest one heads past the rock formations and circles back through head-high bushes. The trail continues past Skull Rock, so keep a close eye out for the turnoff, which is easily missed. It takes a little imagination to see a skull in the rock, but from the right angle, you can definitely work out two eye sockets and a jawline. You can enjoy scrambling around the rocks and then follow one of the small paths circling back to the main trail and primary loop.

The second half of the loop is a steady descent and mostly follows Temescal Canyon Creek. When the creek is running, you'll cross a bridge that offers a nice view of a small cascading falls and enjoy the babbling of the water as you hike. As the loop ends, you'll pass a small area with activities like archery and high ropes courses which can be booked for special programs and retreats.

TURN-BY-TURN DIRECTIONS

1. At the end of the parking lot, keep to the left on a small, paved trail in the direction of the Temescal Ridge Trail. Take a set of steps on the left leading up to an intersection of three trails; take the middle trail leading up and slightly to the right. This is the Temescal Ridge Trail in the direction of Skull Rock.

2. At 0.7 miles, keep slightly right following the direction indicated by the arrow.

3. At 0.9 miles, turn right to stay on the Temescal Ridge Trail.

4. At 1.1 miles, keep left, ignoring a trail spur on the right.

5. At 1.5 miles, continue straight, ignoring the Bienveneda Trail on the left; then, at the intersection with the Temescal Canyon Trail, keep left (the opposite direction from the waterfall). This begins the Skull Rock diversion.

6. At 1.7 miles, continue to the right, ignoring a small trail spur on the left.

7. At 2.1 miles, take a small rocky trail spur on the left that winds up through bushes. This leads to the back of Skull Rock.

8. At 2.2 miles, after circling Skull Rock to fully appreciate it from all angles, follow a small, rocky path in front and slightly to the left of Skull Rock. This leads back to the main trail. From here, turn right and proceed back to the loop trail.

9. At 2.7 miles, when you reach the intersection in Step 5, continue straight for the waterfall on the Temescal Canyon Trail.

10. At 3.1 miles, cross a bridge over a creek and the small Temescal Falls.

11. At 3.9 miles, the trail crosses the creek and becomes slightly unclear. Follow the creek for around 0.1 miles to reach the high ropes course center. Skirt above and to the right of the course space.

12. At 4.4 miles, reach the intersection in Step 1 and head down the stairs on the left back to the parking lot.

FIND THE TRAILHEAD

From Santa Monica, take CA-1 N (otherwise known as Highway 1 or the PCH) for approximately 3.5 miles and turn right on Temescal Canyon Rd. Proceed for 1.3 miles, continuing straight into Temescal Gateway Park. The road narrows when entering the park and there are several different parking areas. Pass a parking fee station and enter the main parking lot just before the Temescal camp store and the parking area reserved for the retreat center. Park here. The trailhead is at the end of the reserved parking area.

On public transportation, take the Number 9 bus from 4th St. and Santa Monica Blvd. for Pacific Palisades. Get off at the stop for Sunset WB and Temescal Canyon NS, then walk up Temescal Canyon Rd. past the parking areas to the trailhead.

SANTA MONICA BREW WORKS

Voted the best local craft brewery in the Westside, Downtown, and East L.A. region by the *Los Angeles Times* in 2022 and 2023, Santa Monica Brew Works is Santa Monica's first and only craft brewery. Thanks to a small group of locals including co-founder, president, and CEO Scott Francis, the brewery began operations in 2014 and opened its taproom in 2016. Head brewer Avery Colomb fell in love with brewing while in medical school on the East Coast when his future wife got him a five-gallon homebrew kit. He started brewing professionally in 2018 and joined the Santa Monica Brew Works team in 2021.

Digging into the local Santa Monica beach vacation vibes, the brewery specializes in easy-drinking brews. This includes the refreshing Stomped Lemonade Shandy, which is a collaboration with the Santa Monica-based business Hot Dog on a Stick. The shandy combines Hot Dog on a Stick's famous "hand-stomped lemonade" with Santa Monica Brew Works' classic 310 blonde ale for a balanced and approachable drink.

LAND MANAGER

Topanga State Park
20828 Entrada Rd.
Topanga, CA 90265
(310) 455-2465
www.parks.ca.gov/?page_id=629
Map: www.mrca.ca.gov/wp-content/uploads/2018/02/temescal -2017-1.pdf

BREWERY/RESTAURANT

Santa Monica Brew Works
1920 Colorado Avenue, Suite C
Santa Monica, CA 90404
(310) 828-7629
www.santamonicabrewworks.com/

Distance from trailhead: 5.7 miles

TOWSLEY CANYON

EXPLORE A DEEP SLOT CANYON AND NATURAL TAR PITS

NEWHALL

▷⋯ STARTING POINT	⋯✕ DESTINATION
TOWSLEY CANYON PARK PARKING LOT	**TOWSLEY GORGE NARROWS**
🍺 BREWERY	🁢 HIKE TYPE
POCOCK BREWING COMPANY	**MODERATE** 🚶
🐾 DOG FRIENDLY	📅 SEASON
YES (LEASH REQUIRED)	**YEAR-ROUND**
💲 FEES	🕐 DURATION
NONE	**2 HOURS 50 MIN.**
⛰ MAP REFERENCE	↦ LENGTH
ED DAVIS PARK MOUNTAINS RECREATION & CONSERVATION AUTHORITY	**6.9 MILES** (LOLLIPOP LOOP)
🔍 HIGHLIGHTS	〰 ELEVATION GAIN
SLOT CANYON, TAR PITS, VIEWS	**1,499 FT**

SURFING HIPPOS HAZY IPA

7.5 % ALCOHOL CONTENT

 HAZY STRAW

 CITRUS

 GRAPEFRUIT, STONE FRUIT

BITTERNESS

SWEETNESS

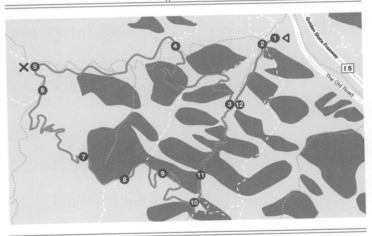

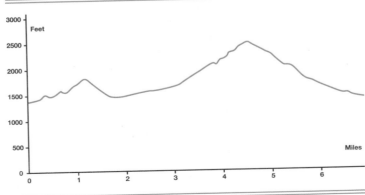

HIKE DESCRIPTION

 Discover this diverse trail through Towsley and Wiley canyons with several fascinating geologic attractions including bubbling tar pits and a slot-like canyon. Posthike, head into town for a tasty brew from Pocock Brewing Co.

The Towsley Canyon Loop Trail mostly travels through the Ed Davis Park in Towsley Canyon. Santa Monica Mountains Conservancy purchased this land in 1989 with legislative help from Republican State Senator Ed Davis. When Davis retired in 1992, the conservancy renamed Towsley Canyon Park "Ed Davis Park in Towsley Canyon." While Davis was famously opposed to environmentalism, he supported the creation of parks for recreational use. In a way, the park's name commemorates a time when it was a bridge between otherwise polarized political opponents.

Our hike begins at the free lot close to the park entrance. You'll follow a road for several hundred feet and then turn off onto the dirt single-track trail leading into Wiley Canyon. The trail connects to a small creek and leads through lush purple sage bushes and wild mustard.

Around the half-mile mark, you'll reach the beginning of the loop. We'll take the loop counterclockwise and start up the first climb of the day. The trail is slightly overgrown with prickly plants and white and purple sage, monkeyflower, and purple elegant clarkia, so long pants will make your experience more comfortable.

A little past the one-mile mark, you'll reach an unassuming high point and then make a brief but steep descent through mixed chaparral, coastal sage scrub, and dispersed oak trees. At the bottom, you'll find an information bulletin with a trail map and a shaded grassy knoll, a babbling creek, a picnic table, a water fountain, and a Spanish-style ranch house called Towsley Lodge. From here, you'll start hiking through Towsley Canyon proper. After leading you through the canyon for around a mile, the trail approaches the Towsley Gorge Narrows—a channel with tall sedimentary rock rising high overhead on either side, Towsley Creek running through the middle, and dappled sunlight peeking through cottonwood and walnut trees. The channel is reminiscent of the famous Narrows in Utah's Zion National Park, though on a smaller scale.

Once you leave the Narrows, you'll face the strenuous climb out of the canyon. This is the hardest part of the hike but offers stunning views of the canyon and an enchanting combination of wildflowers like golden yarrow, purple sage, and speckled clarkia.

After reaching the high point of the trail, you'll descend into Wiley Canyon and meet up with Wiley Creek. Along the side of the trail, you'll see several black tar pits. Here, oil rises naturally from fractures in the rock

layers below—if you look closely, you can see the pits bubbling! Continuing along the creek, the trail meets up with the start of the loop and then leads you back to the parking area.

TURN-BY-TURN DIRECTIONS

1. From the main parking lot, head down the wide paved trail.
2. At 0.1 miles, veer left off the main road onto the Canyon View Loop Trail.
3. At 0.5 miles, just before a small sign reading "Trail," turn right onto a clear unmarked trail. There is a faint trail on the right around 50 feet before the correct turn; ignore this. For the next mile, ignore all smaller trails turning left or right and continue on the better-defined Towsley Canyon View Loop Trail.
4. At 1.7 miles, come to an information bulletin for Ed Davis Park in Towsley Canyon. Towsley Lodge will be on the left. After the bulletin, cross a bridge over a small creek and come out onto a wide gravel-road intersection. Turn left to stay on the Towsley Canyon View Loop Trail. Continue on this medium-width path for 0.9 miles, ignoring any smaller trail spurs.

5. At 2.7 miles, reach the Narrows and start walking through the canyon. Keep to the left of the creek, following a trail directly next to the rock.

6. At 2.9 miles, leave the Narrows and keep left for the signposted "Trail," which will start to switchback up the canyon.

7. At 4.3 miles, keep right on the more clearly established trail, ignoring a small trail spur on the left.

8. At an unmarked fork at 4.6 miles, keep right, staying level with the trail and ignoring the trail going downhill to the left. About 20 feet further, continue straight, ignoring another unmarked trail that doubles back on the right.

9. At 5.1 miles, come to a small, unmarked fork. Both paths here lead to the same destination, but the one on the right has switchbacks and is less steep, while the left-hand path goes straight down; take the less steep path on the right to reduce erosion on the trail.

10. At 5.7 miles, reach the convergence of two small creeks and a small, broken-up trail on the right. Keep left, going down the steep hill and along the creek.

11. At 5.9 miles, reach a large bubbling tar pit on the left side of the trail. Continue downhill on the main trail.

12. At 6.4 miles, reach the beginning of the loop and continue straight to return to the parking lot.

FIND THE TRAILHEAD

From Old Orchard Park in Santa Clarita, head west on Lyons Ave. After 0.7 miles, turn left onto Wiley Canyon Rd. After 1.1 miles, turn right onto Calgrove Blvd.; proceed for 0.3 miles, passing under Highway 5. On the other side of Highway 5, Calgrove Blvd. turns into The Old Road. After 0.1 miles on The Old Road, turn right onto Towsley Canyon Rd. and go through the gated area, entering Ed Davis Park in Towsley Canyon. The main parking area is ahead on the right.

POCOCK BREWING COMPANY

Brothers-in-law Todd Tisdell and Geoff Pocock independently got homebrew kits one Christmas in the mid-2000s and started home-brewing together. As the pair got better at it, their entrepreneurial spirit kicked in, and in October 2015, with their wives' and community support, the pair opened Pocock Brewing Co. Pocock is an English surname, and the brothers-in-law draw on their English heritage to create "English meets West Coast"–style beers—though with 20 to 25 different brews always on tap, they offer many other styles as well.

One of the brewery's staples is the Surfing Hippos New England Hazy IPA, which has a classic juicy taste with a hint of sweetness. The name Surfing Hippos comes from the Netflix documentary *Our Great National Parks,* which features a herd of hippos in Gabon that bodysurf up the coast.

LAND MANAGER

Mountains Recreation & Conservation Authority
24335 The Old Road
Newhall, CA 91321
(323) 221-9944
www.mrca.ca.gov/parks/park-listing/ed-davis-park-in-towsley-canyon/
Map: www.mrca.ca.gov/wp-content/uploads/2018/02/Towsley.
Mullally-1.pdf

BREWERY/RESTAURANT

Pocock Brewing Company
24907 Avenue Tibbitts, Suite B
Santa Clarita, CA 91355
(661) 775-4899
www.pocockbrewing.com/

Distance from trailhead: 7.0 miles

TRAIL CANYON FALLS

HIKE ALONG A CREEK TO A PLUNGING WATERFALL

TUJUNGA

▷⋯ STARTING POINT	⋯✗ DESTINATION
TRAIL CANYON TRAIL PARKING	**TRAIL CANYON FALLS**
🍺 BREWERY	🎛 HIKE TYPE
LINCOLN BEER COMPANY	**MODERATE**
🐾 DOG FRIENDLY	📅 SEASON
YES (LEASH REQUIRED)	**DECEMBER–MAY**
$ FEES	🕐 DURATION
NO	**2 HOURS 40 MIN.**
⛰ MAP REFERENCE	↦ LENGTH
ANGELES NATIONAL FOREST	**5.5 MILES** (ROUND TRIP)
🔍 HIGHLIGHTS	〰 ELEVATION GAIN
WATERFALL, WILDFLOWERS	**1,043 FEET**

**RAILSPLITTER
RED ALE**

 DARK AMBER

 **ROASTY,
COFFEE**

 **MALTY,
COFFEE,
DATE**

BITTERNESS   **SWEETNESS**

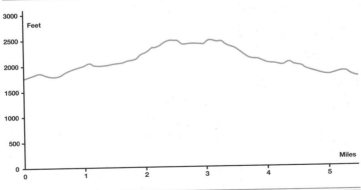

HIKE DESCRIPTION

Venture through Big Tujunga Canyon and Trail Canyon, navigating numerous creek crossings to a roaring waterfall. Return like royalty and enjoy a refreshing brew in a Hollywood-style castle structure at Lincoln Beer Company.

Originally part of the San Gabriel Timberland Reserve, which was created in 1892, this remote part of Angeles National Forest boasts 360-degree views of mountains and engulfs you in a picturesque canyon—though due to the plunging walls of the gorge, don't expect to have service throughout the trail. (So be sure to download everything you need before you head out!) Encompassing over 650,000 acres of land (about a quarter of Los Angeles County), Angeles National Forest has an immensely diverse range of offerings and hosts 3.5 to 4 million visitors annually, thanks to its vicinity to LA.

As you drive along winding mountain roads to the trailhead, you'll leave behind the cityscape and trade it for green mountains covered with dense chaparral. You'll park on the side of Big Tujunga Canyon Road and hike up a dirt road to the former parking area, where you'll find a national forest bulletin with rules for the area and a description of potential hazards. A couple hundred feet beyond the former parking lot, you'll come upon the first of several creek crossings and pass a few private houses. Depending on the water level, a couple of the crossings may require wading through knee-deep water, but many of them have strategically placed logs or rocks to help you stay dry. After the first crossing, the trail narrows for the rest of the hike.

You'll keep to the canyon creek bed for around a mile, navigating various crossings amid a lush riparian habitat featuring alders, sycamores, and oak trees. Just under two miles in, you'll start hiking up above the valley floor, steadily climbing around 400 feet in 0.4 miles. As you climb, you'll be rewarded with views up and down the canyon and patches of yellow, orange, purple, and white wildflowers blooming next to the trail and on the hillsides.

Around two and a half miles from the trailhead, after a turn in the canyon, you'll get your first view of the waterfall below you on the right. The singletrack trail curves around towards the falls and then descends, steep and rocky, to the pool at the base of the falls. The descent is manageable but challenging; a static rope is there to hold onto if you need it. The reward is direct access to the falls and a shallow pool to enjoy a snack by before heading back.

TURN-BY-TURN DIRECTIONS

1. From the parking area, take the wide road on the left following the sign and arrows for the Trail Canyon trailhead (TRHD).
2. At 0.2 miles, veer right on Trail Canyon Road and Trail Canyon Falls Trail.
3. At 0.4 miles, reach the former parking area on the right. Follow a brown post with yellow letters and an arrow reading "TRAIL" pointing slightly left towards a bulletin. Follow this wide trail past a yellow metal gate.
4. At 0.5 miles, you'll reach the first river crossing. After crossing, turn left and follow the arrows for "TRAIL." Stay on this main trail, ignoring any side roads—these are private.
5. Follow the clear trail along the creek, making another eight crossings over the next mile and a half.
6. At 2.5 miles, find a steep, unmarked trail on the right and look for the rope to help support your scramble down. The waterfall will be directly on the left after the descent. Return the way you came.

FIND THE TRAILHEAD

From the Sunland Blvd. exit on I-210, head east on Sunland Blvd. Continue for 0.3 miles and then merge onto Foothill Blvd. Proceed for 0.4 miles to Oro Vista Ave., where you'll turn left. After 0.9 miles, Oro Vista Ave. turns into Big Tujunga Canyon Rd. Stay on Big Tujunga Canyon Rd. for 4.4 miles. The trailside parking consists of two separate dirt pull-outs on the left.

LINCOLN BEER COMPANY

Owners Patrick and Laura Dunn hadn't intended to open their brewery in a castle. Their original plan was to run a tiny five-barrel operation in a shipping container in a parking lot on Lincoln Boulevard in Santa Monica—hence the name, Lincoln Beer Company. However, with city permits and other hoops to jump, they realized a larger location would be easier and set out to find a place. When they first saw the castle, they wrote it off, but after further searching, they realized it was exactly what they needed. The building was never actually a castle, though; it was built in the eighties by real estate developer Gary Bandy, who decorated Burbank with numerous castle-like structures because he preferred them to drab industrial buildings. The brewery officially opened in late 2017.

The fifteen-barrel castle brewery is decorated in a fun, industrial style. Its various murals include a black-and-white "sexy" Abe Lincoln in a "paint me like one of your French girls" pose. The beers are flavorful and experimental, and include the Railsplitter Red Ale, which won silver medals for American-style amber/red ale at the 2022 Great American Beer Festival and San Diego International Beer Competition.

LAND MANAGER

Angeles National Forest
701 N. Santa Anita Ave.
Arcadia, CA 91006
(626) 574-1613
www.fs.usda.gov/angeles
Map: www.fs.usda.gov/recarea/angeles/recreation/hiking/recarea/?recid=41940&actid=50

BREWERY/RESTAURANT

Lincoln Beer Company
3083 Lima St.
Burbank, CA 91504
(818) 861-7169
www.lincolnbeercompany.com/

Distance from trailhead: 12.2 miles

GRIFFITH PARK HOLLYWOOD SIGN

SEE THE ICONIC HOLLYWOOD SIGN!

LOS ANGELES

▷⋯ STARTING POINT	⋯✗ DESTINATION
GRIFFITH PARK MERRY-GO-ROUND LOWER LOT PARKING	**HOLLYWOOD SIGN**
🍺 BREWERY	🗺 HIKE TYPE
PAPERBACK BREWING COMPANY	**MODERATE** 🚶
🐾 DOG FRIENDLY	📅 SEASON
YES (LEASH REQUIRED)	**YEAR-ROUND**
$ FEES	🕐 DURATION
NONE	**3 HOURS 40 MIN.**
⛰ MAP REFERENCE	↦ LENGTH
GRIFFITH PARK MAP	**8.1 MILES** (LOLLIPOP LOOP)
🔍 HIGHLIGHTS	〰 ELEVATION GAIN
PEAK BAGGING, CITY OVERLOOKS, HOLLYWOOD SIGN	**1,975 FEET**

BUNNY WITH A CHAINSAW HAZY IPA

8.2% ALCOHOL CONTENT

 HONEY

 FLORAL, GRAPEFRUIT

 HOPPY, DRY

BITTERNESS   SWEETNESS

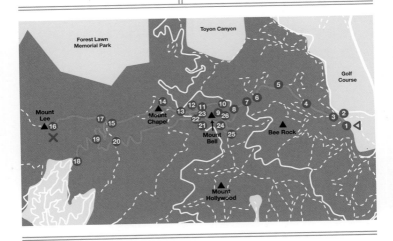

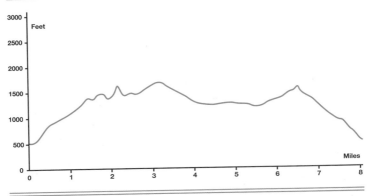

HIKE DESCRIPTION

See the Hollywood Sign from above and below and escape to more secluded trails in the park for a healthy dose of peak bagging and expansive overlooks. Posthike, head over to Paperback Brewing Co. for a pint of a comically named brew like Bunny with a Chainsaw or Satan Wears Pajamas.

The Hollywood Sign might be the best-known symbol of Southern California, and it's definitely worth seeing at least once. While there are far less demanding hikes that will gain you views of the sign, this longer excursion offers multiple views of it and lets you experience some of the wild and undeveloped parts of Griffith Park.

At 4,210 acres, Griffith Park is one of the largest municipal parks with urban wilderness in the United States. This land—along with most of the rest of LA—was originally home to the Chumash and Gabrielino-Tongva Native Americans, and many still live in LA. While the park now features a number of manicured picnic areas, playgrounds, and paved trails, it also has wilder sections with native chaparral ecosystems, mountainous peaks, and diverse wildlife. For ten years up until December 2022, a male mountain lion known as P-22 lived in Griffith Park, joining the ranks of celebrities living in LA. Fondly referred to as the "Lion King," "Hollywood Cat," and "Brad Pitt of mountain lions," P-22 was compassionately euthanized at the estimated age of twelve after being hit by a car while suffering from heart and kidney disease.

For this hike, you'll begin walking through one of the landscaped picnic and park areas and then head up steeply on an unmarked singletrack dirt trail. The trail leads you through a wild and hilly chaparral

landscape. In spring, yellow brittlebush flowers, California poppies, and other wildflowers line many of the smaller trails. Year-round, oak trees, laurel sumac, and toyon offer occasional bits of shade, though much of the trail is fairly exposed to the sun. Throughout, you'll alternate between more populated trails and quieter, unpaved, more adventurous offshoots that bring you to various peaks and viewpoints. Overall, the trail is heavily trafficked, but following these offshoots, you'll be able to enjoy some solitary moments even on a sunny Saturday afternoon.

After some intense elevation gain and two different summits (the second reached by some light scrambling), you'll join the main paved trail up to Mount Lee, just above the Hollywood Sign, where you'll enjoy views of the various peaks in Griffith park and all of LA sprawled out below. From here, you'll head back down along the primary paved Hollywood Sign route to get the classic view of the sign from below before starting on the back half of the loop.

There is a huge amount of history surrounding Griffith Park, and many movies have included the Hollywood Sign. You can find out more in the book *Discovering Griffith Park: A Local's Guide*.

TURN-BY-TURN DIRECTIONS

1. Starting from the parking lot, head north through a picnic area.
2. At 0.1 miles, on the far side of the picnic area, follow a narrow, unmarked dirt trail uphill between a paved road and a wide dirt road with a white metal gate.
3. At a small intersection at 0.2 miles, continue straight.
4. At a main intersection at 0.4 miles, cross the main trail and continue straight up a steep, rocky, unmarked trail.
5. At 0.7 miles, join the wide Bill Eckert Trail and continue straight.
6. At 0.9 miles, just before passing a large water tank on the right, veer off the main trail to the right onto a small path traversing the side of the hill. You'll pass directly next to the water tank.
7. At 1.0 miles, climb a long set of stairs to a wide paved trail and a water fountain. On the paved trail, continue to the right.
8. At 1.2 miles, take a dirt trail, veering off to the left on the N. Trail for Mt. Hollywood Summit.
9. At an intersection at 1.4 miles, go right on the N. Trail in the direction of Vista Del Valle Dr. and Mt. Hollywood Dr. This is the beginning of the loop.
10. At 1.5 miles, veer slightly left heading in the direction of Mt. Hollywood Dr.
11. At 1.7 miles, take a sharp right onto a small unmarked trail leading uphill.
12. At 1.8 miles, reach Mt. Baby Bell summit.
13. At 1.9 miles, come out onto a wide paved path and go left. Cross this path and almost immediately follow a wide dirt path on the right. Around 100 feet down this trail, take a small trail spur on the left heading uphill; keep right at the next two forks going up the mountain.

14. After a mild scramble, reach Mt. Chapel at 2.1 miles.

15. Head downhill on the other side of Mt. Chapel to an unmarked fork at 2.5 miles. Go right; the trail will quickly lead downhill to a wide paved road. Follow this road uphill to the right and stay on it until it dead-ends at Mt. Lee, just above the Hollywood Sign.

16. From the Mt. Lee summit at 3.1 miles, start returning on the road you came up on.

17. At 3.7 miles, continue curving right on the main paved road rather than going back on the trail you came on. Stay on the main paved road, ignoring a wide dirt road on the left.

18. At 4.4 miles, take a sharp right onto a steep dirt trail spur. This will intersect a paved road and you'll get the classic view of the Hollywood Sign. Once you've gotten the photos and views you want, retrace your steps back up towards the wide dirt road you ignored in the previous step.

19. At 4.8 miles, take the wide dirt road on the right.

20. At 5.1 miles, continue straight on the Mulholland Trail in the direction of the Brush Canyon Trail. Over the next 0.9 miles, ignore all turn-offs and continue straight.

21. At 6.0 miles, go left on Mt. Hollywood Drive.

22. At 6.1 miles, take the dirt path heading up to the right. In around 150 feet, reach a T-junction and turn right.

23. At 6.2 miles, reach the junction from step 11. This time, keep straight on the unmarked gravel path.

24. At 6.4 miles, take a small trail spur on the right for Taco Peak. At the top, follow the trail back down to the main path.

25. At 6.5 miles, converge with the main path and follow a small, unmarked, less defined trail straight ahead going steeply downhill. After around 150 feet, emerge onto another main path and turn left.

26. At 6.7 miles, come to a T-junction and turn right on the North Trail in the direction of Vista Del Valle Dr. and Bee Rock. This closes the loop; retrace your steps back to the parking lot from step 9.

FIND THE TRAILHEAD

From downtown Los Angeles, take US-101 S.; proceed for 0.7 miles and then keep left at the fork to continue on San Bernardino Fwy., following signs for I-10 E/San Bernardino. After 0.7 miles, take the exit for State St. towards Soto St. Then turn right onto N. State St. and take the next right to merge onto I-5 N. Continue for 6.1 miles and then take Exit 141B towards Griffith Park Dr. After 0.3 miles, turn right onto Crystal Springs Dr. and proceed for 0.8 miles. At the next intersection, turn left onto Fire Rd. and continue through Lot One on the right and into Lot Two. The trail starts at the end of this parking lot.

PAPERBACK BREWING COMPANY

Tucked into a World War II–era aircraft hangar in an industrial part of Glendale, Paperback Brewing has been making a name for itself with creative beer names, pulp fiction artwork, and, of course, delicious beers. Co-owners Brandon Monroe and Chris Cesnek opened the brewery in 2020 just as the pandemic shutdowns hit. The two had been managing their own homebrewing for years out of Monroe's garage, which earned the nickname "The Lab." After years of experimenting in The Lab, they took the leap and opened their own official brewery.

The taproom provides a relaxed, vintage atmosphere with leather booth benches, lounge chairs, and various knickknacks decorating the walls. Out front, be sure to grab a smashed burger from the Bun & Blanket food truck. Paperback touts a hop-forward approach to its beers, particularly with its bestseller, the dank and hoppy double hazy Bunny With A Chainsaw IPA.

LAND MANAGER

Los Angeles Department of Parks
4730 Crystal Springs
Drive Los Angeles, CA 90027
(323) 644-2050
www.laparks.org/griffithpark/
Map: www.laparks.org/griffithpark/pdf/GriffithParkMap.pdf

BREWERY/RESTAURANT

Paperback Brewing Company
422 Magnolia Ave
Glendale, CA 91204
(818) 484-5079
www.paperback.la/

Distance from trailhead: 3.1 miles

WHITTIER HILL

A STEEP CLIMB TO A WATER TOWER WITH GREAT VIEWS

WHITTIER

▷⋯ STARTING POINT	⋯✕ DESTINATION
HELLMAN PARK TRAILHEAD	**WHITTIER HILL**
🍺 BREWERY	🔳 HIKE TYPE
BREWJERÍA COMPANY	**MODERATE** 🚶
🐾 DOG FRIENDLY	📅 SEASON
YES (LEASH REQUIRED)	**YEAR-ROUND**
$ FEES	🕐 DURATION
NONE	**1 HOURS 30 MIN.**
⛰ MAP REFERENCE	↦ LENGTH
POSTED AT TRAILHEAD	**3.7 MILES** (ROUND TRIP)
👁 HIGHLIGHTS	〰 ELEVATION GAIN
BIRD WATCHING, WATER TOWER, LATINO-OWNED BREWERY	**876 FEET**

6.2 %
ALCOHOL
CONTENT

TOMO LA FLOR PALE ALE

 ROUGE

 FLORAL, FRUITY

 HIBISCUS, FLORAL

BITTERNESS

SWEETNESS

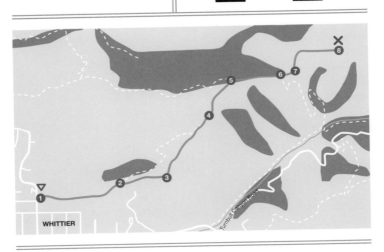

WHITTIER

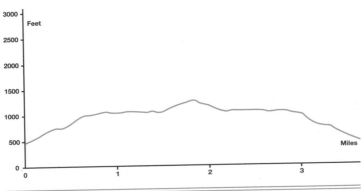

HIKE DESCRIPTION

Get a workout on this steep hike up wide trails to a graffiti-covered water tower and expansive views of Los Angeles, the San Gabriel Mountains, and the Santa Ana Mountains. Then head to nearby Brewjería Company for refreshing brews and regular rotating food trucks.

Hellman Park—where this trail begins—is part of the approximately 3,870 acres of open space managed by the Puente Hills Habitat Preservation Authority. The open space also makes up part of the Puente–Chino Hills Wildlife Corridor. Wildlife corridors connect pockets of wildlife habitat in heavily urbanized areas like Los Angeles so that wild animals can move from one area to another and maintain healthier populations. This is particularly important for species that have a wide range like bobcats and mountain lions.

This hike is on the shorter side at 3.7 miles, but it's nothing to scoff at with its 876 feet of elevation gain. Plus, the landscape of sage scrub, chaparral, and grasslands is almost entirely exposed to direct sun. Our route largely follows a wide and well-trafficked fire road, however, so it's a safe option for beginner and intermediate hikers looking for a good training trail.

From the trailhead, the fire road kicks off with several hundred feet of climbing over the first half mile. Lining the trail, you'll see plants like prickly pear cactuses, wild mustard, and milk thistle. While the wild mustard and milk thistle are invasive, the prickly pear cactus is a native species known for its flat, prickly paddles, vibrant red, pink, yellow, and orange flowers, and edible fruit (after getting rid of the spines!). The prickly pear cactus typically blooms from late spring to early summer and is a gem in the landscape.

After the first mile along the fire road, you'll get a brief respite from the steep climbing. In the spring, this section of the trail bursts into color with wildflowers like lupine, hairy vetch, and deerweed. A little past the one-mile mark, you'll meet the Rattlesnake Ridge Trail and hike along a ridgeline. Looking northwest, you'll see a terracotta-roofed pagoda on one of the nearby hillsides; this is the Fo Guang Shan Buddhist Columbarium. Part of the Rose Hills Memorial Park and Mortuary, the columbarium—a place where funeral urns are stored—was built in 1999, replicating the architecture of ancient Chinese palaces.

From here, you'll also see the Turnbull Canyon water tower ahead at the end of the final half-mile uphill push. Covered in graffiti and satellite dishes, the striking water tower looks like a modern sculpture. On a clear day, the views from the summit stretch out over Los Angeles to the surrounding mountains and the ocean.

TURN-BY-TURN DIRECTIONS

1. From the information bulletin, head up the main fire road on the Peppergrass Trail.
2. At 0.4 miles, continue straight on the Peppergrass Trail, ignoring the Mariposa Trail on the left.
3. At 0.6 miles, the trail levels off briefly and comes to an overlook from which you can see the city and the trail you've climbed thus far. Continue on the Peppergrass Trail.
4. At 1.0 miles, keep right to stay on the Peppergrass Trail, ignoring a narrow, unmarked trail on the left.
5. At 1.2 miles, reach a T-junction and turn right onto the Rattlesnake Ridge Trail.
6. At 1.4 miles, continue straight on the Rattlesnake Ridge Trail, ignoring the Sumac Trail on the right.
7. At 1.5 miles, keep right, heading uphill on the main unmarked trail towards the water tower.
8. At 1.8 miles, reach Whittier Hill and the Turnbull Canyon water tower. Return the way you came.

FIND THE TRAILHEAD

From the East Los Angeles Library and Belvedere Park Lake, head east on E 3rd St. After 0.3 miles, take a slight right onto E Beverly Blvd. and proceed for 7.8 miles. At the intersection with Greenleaf Ave., turn left. After 0.1 miles, just after the next intersection, the trailhead will be on the right. Parking can be a challenge here—there is a small parking lot for the trailhead, but it's often closed off and a large portion of nearby street parking is permit-only.

There are a few bus options that can get you close to the trailhead as well. Either take the Route 10 Whittier Blvd. bus, get off at Philadelphia and Milton, and walk about a mile north on Greenleaf Ave., or take the Route 7 bus, get off at Beverly Blvd. and Greenleaf Ave., and walk about 0.2 miles north on Greenleaf Ave.

BREWJERÍA COMPANY

Brewjería Company started up in 2010 in co-founder and president Agustin Ruelas' kitchen as a brew club for a group of friends and family. The group experimented with brewing and threw parties to share their beer with the wider community. Over time, the parties became unmanageable, so the team started donating their beer to nonprofit events instead. By 2018, they were doing events almost every weekend on top of regular full-time jobs, and it was all becoming unsustainable. So, with the community's help, in November 2019 Brewjería Company opened its doors as an official brewery. Reflecting the teams' Latino and Mexican American roots, the name Brewjería combines the English word "brew" with the Spanish word "brujería," which means witchcraft. The brewery still works closely to support many local nonprofits.

One of its popular brews, Tomo la Flor, uses hibiscus flowers and draws inspiration from the Mexican drink agua de Jamaica. The name Tomo la Flor loosely translates as "I drink the flower" and is a play on words on the popular Selena song "Como la Flor" or "Like the Flower."

LAND MANAGER

Puente Hills Habitat Preservation Authority
7333 Greenleaf Avenue, First Floor
Whittier, CA 90602
(562) 945-9003
www.habitatauthority.org/
Map: www.habitatauthority.org/wp-content/uploads/2020/09/
Map_Sycamore_Hellman-2018.pdf

BREWERY/RESTAURANT

Brewjería Company
4937 Durfee Ave
Pico Rivera, CA 90660
(562) 641-9720
www.brewjeriacompany.com/

Distance from trailhead: 3.1 miles

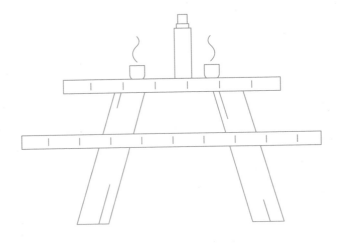

FIRST WATER VIA MT. WILSON TRAIL

AN ENCHANTING STOP ON THE TRAIL TO MT. WILSON

SIERRA MADRE

▷··· STARTING POINT	···✕ DESTINATION
MOUNT WILSON TRAIL PARK	**FIRST WATER**
🍺 BREWERY	🔃 HIKE TYPE
RT ROGERS BREWING COMPANY	**MODERATE**
🐾 DOG FRIENDLY	📅 SEASON
YES (LEASH SUGGESTED)	**OCTOBER—JUNE**
$ FEES	⊘ DURATION
NONE	**2 HOURS 15 MIN.**
⟁ MAP REFERENCE	↦ LENGTH
POSTED ALONG TRAIL	**4.0 MILES** (ROUND TRIP)
🔍 HIGHLIGHTS	〰 ELEVATION GAIN
WATERFALL, CREEKSIDE, WILDLIFE	**1,089 FEET**

THE GOLD SPINNER'S HEFEWEIZEN

5.9 %
ALCOHOL CONTENT

DARK STRAW

ORANGE, BANANA

BANANA, CLOVE

BITTERNESS

SWEETNESS

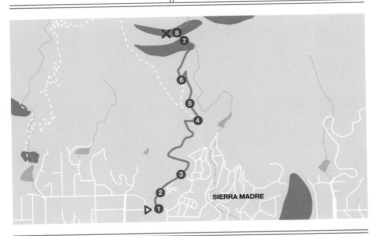

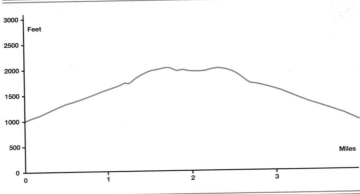

HIKE DESCRIPTION

Hike a portion of the challenging Mount Wilson Trail to an ethereal clearing along the Little Santa Anita Creek. Afterwards, head to RT Rogers Brewing Company's homey spot in downtown Sierra Madre for a refreshing Hefeweizen.

A note on wildlife: This trail is known for black bear sightings, so come prepared. While no signs say dogs must be on leash, I would highly recommend keeping your dog leashed for its own safety.

This moderate hike takes us to First Water, which is named because it's the first water source hikers reach along the trail. First Water is only the first stop along the strenuous trek up Mt. Wilson, but makes for a rewarding day all on its own. The Mt. Wilson Trail is a historic one: originally created by the Gabrielino-Tongva Tribe, it's home to one of the oldest trail races in California. You can learn more about the trail's history from the Richardson House and Lizzy's Trail Inn museums at the start of the hike.

From the Mount Wilson Trail Park, you'll head up a residential street called Mt. Wilson Trail until you reach the beginning of the official Mount Wilson Trail, marked with an archway and trail map. The trail is relentlessly uphill and very challenging in the summer heat, but features scenic canyon views up and down Little Santa Anita Canyon.

At around the one-mile mark, you'll cross a short wooden bridge. This is part of trail work undertaken after the Bobcat Fire in 2020, which burned over 115,000 acres and severely damaged many of the trails in this region (some areas remain closed as of summer 2023). Just past the bridge, keep your eyes peeled towards the base of the canyon for aerial views of Little Santa Anita Creek tumbling over smooth gray rocks. If you're a fan of waterfall views, bring binoculars or a zoom lens to get a proper look at these plunging falls.

The trail continues to switchback up the side of the canyon, which can be brutal on sunny days, but the low vegetation also makes for stunning views out to Sierra Madre and the larger Los Angeles area. In the spring and summer, you may also enjoy various wildflowers, such as the showy penstemon and scarlet larkspur, both native species only found in Southern and Baja California.

Just before the two-mile mark, you'll reach the turn-off for First Water diverging from the main trail that continues to Orchard Camp and Mt. Wilson. The path winds down to the creekside, sheltered by a lush canopy of oak, sycamore, and alder trees. With the sun filtering through the canopy and the gurgling creek flowing over and around rocks, the clearing is a magical respite from the sunny trail. Take your time to pause for a snack and explore up and down the creek—if you follow it down approximately 100 feet, you'll see the water flow together into a single narrow channel through light gray rock to make its way down the canyon.

TURN-BY-TURN DIRECTIONS

1. From Mount Wilson Trail Park, head up to the corner with the Richardson House and Lizzy's Trail Inn museums. Turn right and head up Mt. Wilson Trail Rd.
2. At 0.1 miles, reach the archway for the Mount Wilson Trail on the left. Go under the archway and follow the dirt trail.
3. At 0.3 miles, join a wider dirt path and continue straight. Shortly after, you'll pass a bulletin with Mt. Wilson Trail rules and warnings and information about the Mt. Wilson Trail Race. Stay on the main established trail, ignoring any smaller offshoots.
4. At 1.0 miles, reach the signposted Lower Trail Junction. Keep right to stay on the Old Mt. Wilson Trail towards First Water, Orchard Camp, and Mt. Wilson.
5. At 1.1 miles, cross a wooden bridge.
6. At 1.5 miles, pass another signposted turn-off for Charley's New Trail; keep right on the main Mt. Wilson Trail, ignoring Charley's New Trail.
7. At 1.9 miles, keep right on the Mt. Wilson Trail to First Water. Follow the main trail straight, gradually descending to the creekside in approximately 200 feet.
8. At 2.0 miles, after reaching First Water and exploring the area, cross the creek and follow it down approximately 100 feet to see the water flow into a channel of light gray rock. From here, cross the creek again and take a small, steep trail leading back up to the main trail. Return the way you came. (You can also simply retrace your steps from where you meet the creek.)

FIND THE TRAILHEAD

From Old Pasadena, head east on E Colorado Blvd. After 0.2 miles, turn left onto N Marengo Ave. After 0.4 miles, turn right onto Corson St. and immediately keep left to merge onto I-210 E towards San Bernardino. After 5.1 miles on I-210 E, take Exit 31 for Baldwin Ave. At the end of the off-ramp, turn left onto N Baldwin Ave. After 0.1 miles, turn right onto W Foothill Blvd.; proceed for 0.3 miles and then turn left onto San Carlos Rd. After 0.5 miles, continue straight onto S Mountain Trail Ave. After 0.8 miles, the road will curve to the left and become E Mira Monte Ave.; Mount Wilson Trail Park will be immediately on your right. You can park anywhere along the street here.

RT ROGERS BREWING COMPANY

Head brewer Ryan Rogers started homebrewing in his closet at 16 years of age—just as an experiment. He wasn't a beer fan until he was 22, so when he finished a batch, he'd dump it and start over. Eventually, with his parents' approval, he moved his experiments from the closet to the kitchen—and then outside, because the process was so messy. After years of homebrewing as a hobby, Ryan proposed starting a brewery with his parents Joanna and Kelly. After many long discussions with his parents, his brother Jesse, and Jesse's wife Deanna, the family opened RT Rogers Brewing in 2017 with three beers on tap.

Today's small brewery features a cozy, wood-cabin aesthetic complete with old books from Joanna's grandmother's library, red beer tower taps, and seasonal decorations. Each beer comes with a whimsical, fairytale-esque name and artwork hand-drawn by Jesse. The Gold Spinner's Hefeweizen has notes of baking spices when it's freshly brewed. As it ages, it also develops banana notes.

LAND MANAGER

Angeles National Forest
701 N. Santa Anita Ave.
Arcadia, CA 91006
(626) 574-1613
www.fs.usda.gov/angeles
Map: store.avenza.com/products/mount-wilson-angeles-atlas-us-for-est-service-r5-map?queryID=undefined&objectID=36444123889820

BREWERY/RESTAURANT

RT Rogers Brewing Co.
38 E Montecito Ave Unit #1
Sierra Madre, CA 91024
(626) 921-0308
www.rtrbrew.com/

Distance from trailhead: 0.6 miles

MOUNT BLISS

A DEMANDING HIKE TO PANORAMIC MOUNTAIN VIEWS

DUARTE

▷··· STARTING POINT	···✗ DESTINATION
VAN TASSEL TRAILHEAD	**MOUNT BLISS**
🍺 BREWERY	🗺 HIKE TYPE
HOP SECRET BREWING COMPANY	**STRENUOUS**
🐾 DOG FRIENDLY	📅 SEASON
YES (LEASH REQUIRED)	**OCTOBER—JUNE**
$ FEES	🕐 DURATION
NONE	**5 HOURS**
⛰ MAP REFERENCE	↦ LENGTH
POSTED AT TRAILHEAD	**9.6 MILES** (ROUND TRIP)
🔍 HIGHLIGHTS	〰 ELEVATION GAIN
MOUNTAIN VISTAS, WILDFLOWERS	**3,028 FEET**

CLOSE TALKER LAGER

PALE GOLD

BREADY, BISCUIT

LIGHT,
DRY,
TOAST

BITTERNESS   SWEETNESS

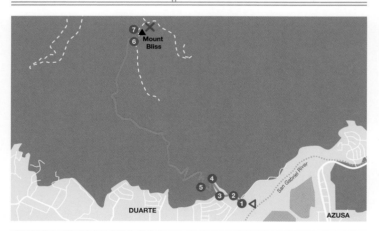

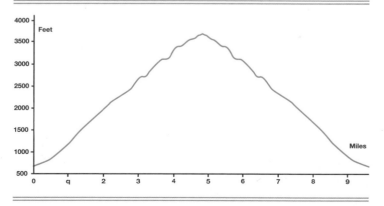

HIKE DESCRIPTION

Get a good workout on a blissful summit hike with gorgeous wild-flowers and mountain views. After this leg-burner, hop over to Hop Secret Brewing Company for a light, refreshing lager.

At 3,720 feet, Mount Bliss isn't the highest peak in the area, but when you've overcome its 3,000 feet of elevation gain, you'll feel a sense of significant accomplishment. In recent years, this area of Angeles National Forest has been hit by several different wildfires, including the Bobcat Fire of 2020, which burned 115,796 acres and was the second-largest wildfire ever recorded in Los Angeles County. Because of the Bobcat Fire, our trail was closed for over two years; the National Forest Service still marks the Van Tassel Motorway as a sensitive and potentially hazardous area. Other nearby areas, including the popular Chantry Flat, remain closed.

The trail begins from the parking area and heads past the Encanto Equestrian Center via a gated dirt road. After passing the Equestrian Center and crossing a seasonal creek, the trail narrows and begins climbing in earnest. From here, you'll have steep climbing and very lit-tle shade coverage for almost the entire rest of the hike—approximately four more miles each way to the summit and back.

Given the steep climbing and intense exposure to the sun, it's best to do this trail during cooler weather or early in the morning. The lack of trees also means you'll get expansive views over Los Angeles and the San Gabriel Mountains. And in the spring and early summer, the trail passes through a variety of colorful wildflowers including deerweed, bush monkeyflower, golden yarrow, and sunflowers.

The wide dirt fire road winds its way up the mountain to a ridgeline that you'll follow up to the top. Cloud inversions are common higher up, which means you might be hiking above the clouds and looking down on them. The last push to the peak leads you off the established fire road and onto a more rugged trail that narrows as you approach the summit. On the final several hundred feet, you'll pass through a field of wildflowers and enjoy open views of the surrounding mountains.

TURN-BY-TURN DIRECTIONS

1. From the trailhead, which features a bulletin map of the Van Tassel Trail, head down the gravel road away from the main paved road on the Van Tassel Trail.

2. At 0.1 miles, pass through a white metal gate.

3. At 0.2 miles, continue straight on the main gravel road, ignoring the Encanto Equestrian Center on the right.

4. At 0.5 miles, follow the trail across the creekbed and start up a switchback on the left.

5. At 0.8 miles, ignore the unmarked trail on the left and keep right on the wide trail going uphill.

6. At 4.6 miles, take a sharp right, continuing uphill on a wide trail. Around 50 feet later, take a sharp left heading uphill under the power lines.

7. At 4.8 miles, reach the summit, which is marked with an American flag. Return the way you came.

FIND THE TRAILHEAD

From Old Pasadena, head east on E Colorado Blvd. After 0.2 miles, turn left onto M Marengo Ave. After 0.4 miles, turn right onto Corson St. and keep left to merge onto I-210 E towards San Bernardino; proceed for 12.1 miles and take Exit 38 for Irwindale Ave. At the end of the off-ramp, turn left onto Irwindale Ave. After 0.3 miles, turn left onto E Foot-hill Blvd. After 0.7 miles, turn right onto Encanto Pkwy. After 1.2 miles, continue straight onto Fish Canyon Rd.; the trailhead is 0.2 miles down Fish Canyon Rd. on the left and features a large map and parking area.

HOP SECRET BREWING COMPANY

Co-owners Chris Thomas and Ky Pedulla took over Hop Secret Brew-ing Company from the previous owner in 2020 and rebranded with a colorful quirky style that expresses their appreciation for video games, Star Wars, and good beer. Thomas, the head brewer, has been homebrewing since 2015 and has a culinary and hospitality background that has helped him in creating his beer recipes. The pair has placed high priority on creating a fun and welcoming space in the taproom, with colorful watercolor artwork lining the walls and arcade machines and video games available for customers to play.

True to the name Hop Secret, the brewery has a hop-forward focus, but it offers a brew for every taste, including the award-winning Close Talker Hells German Lager. This light and bready beer won a silver medal at the 2021 California Craft Brewers Cup. The Close Talker and a Mexican lager are alternately available on tap.

LAND MANAGER

Angeles National Forest
701 N. Santa Anita Ave.
Arcadia, CA 91006
(626) 574-1613
www.fs.usda.gov/angeles
Map: www.fs.usda.gov/detail/angeles/maps-pubs/?cid=FSEPRD631156

BREWERY/RESTAURANT

Hop Secret Brewing Company
162 W Pomona Ave.
Monrovia, CA 91016
(626) 386-5960
www.hopsecretbrewing.com/

Distance from trailhead: 5.1 miles

SAN BERNARDINO

MOUNT BALDY

HIKE THE HIGHEST PEAK IN THE SAN GABRIEL MOUNTAINS

MT BALDY

▷⋯ STARTING POINT	⋯✕ DESTINATION
MT. BALDY TRAILHEAD	**MOUNT BALDY/MOUNT SAN ANTONIO**
🍺 BREWERY	🀫 HIKE TYPE
CLAREMONT CRAFT ALES	**STRENUOUS**
🐾 DOG FRIENDLY	📅 SEASON
YES	**JUNE–OCTOBER**
$ FEES	🕓 DURATION
YES (AMERICA THE BEAUTIFUL)	**7 HOURS**
⛰ MAP REFERENCE	↦ LENGTH
POSTED AT TRAILHEAD	**10.9 MILES** (LOLLIPOP LOOP)
👁 HIGHLIGHTS	〰 ELEVATION GAIN
MOUNTAIN SUMMIT, RIDGELINE	**3,967 FEET**

BALDY PILSNER

 PALE STRAW

 BISCUIT,
BREAD

 LIGHT,
MALTY,
CITRUS

BITTERNESS   SWEETNESS

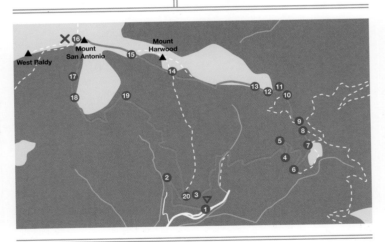

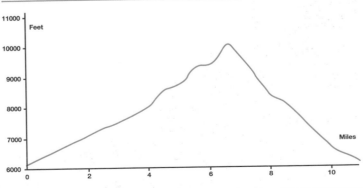

HIKE DESCRIPTION

Take on the hardest hike in this book and an iconic Southern California peak. Then celebrate your accomplishment with a Claremont Craft Ales beer named after the mountain you just climbed.

The mountain generally known as Mount Baldy (10,064 ft) is officially named Mount San Antonio, after Saint Anthony of Padua. "Baldy" was coined by early settlers, who saw the prominent peak from Los Angeles and saw its treeless and often snow-capped top as bald.

The route up Baldy via the Devil's Backbone Trail is by no means the hardest in Southern California and isn't even the longest in this book, but don't be fooled: this hike is no joke. It is long, steep, and tops off at over 10,000 feet, and the unpredictable conditions at the summit can be very different from those at the trailhead. Snow can linger at the top well into June, and you may even see patches in July. In dry conditions, the trail doesn't require any technical expertise, but snow and ice can turn the route into a proper mountaineering outing.

The trail begins by heading up a wide paved road through conifers including Douglas firs and Jeffrey pines. The road continues for half a mile, during which you'll begin to hear water from San Antonio Falls (if it's running). Around the half-mile mark, you'll reach an outstanding view of this 75-foot, multi-tiered falls. There's a small, approximately 0.1-mile trail spur leading to the falls that's a great add-on on the way back if you still have energy.

From here, the trail transitions to a gravel road and steadily gains elevation as it heads up a partially shaded canyon. In the winter, Mt. Baldy is a popular ski resort, so you'll see a chairlift heading up the mountain. On summer weekends, the lift runs a few times a day, and if you want

to shorten your hike, you can take advantage of the ride. Around the 3.5-mile mark, you'll reach the main Baldy resort area and the Top of the Notch restaurant, which has limited opening hours on summer weekends.

From here, you'll follow a chairlift up a steep slope until you get to a signpost for the beginning of the Devil's Backbone Trail—an exposed ridgeline path with steep drop-offs on either side. This is the most treacherous and challenging part of the hike, but also the most rewarding, with unbeatable views looking back at the ridgeline you've just climbed. The final push to the summit features rocky, exposed switchbacks. Once at the summit, take in the 360-degree views and then head down the steep, sunny Baldy Bowl Trail to complete the loop.

Towards the end of the loop, you'll weave through a partly forested section, with chaparral yucca plants dotting the landscape on either side of the trail. These plants take 5 to 8 years to fully mature, at which point they shoot up an 8- to 10-foot stalk with cream or purple flowers in the springtime. The chaparral yucca only flowers once in its lifetime, so consider yourself lucky if you get a glimpse of these fascinating blooming stalks!

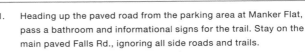

TURN-BY-TURN DIRECTIONS

1. Heading up the paved road from the parking area at Manker Flat, pass a bathroom and informational signs for the trail. Stay on the main paved Falls Rd., ignoring all side roads and trails.

2. At 0.6 miles, reach the lookout towards San Antonio Falls on the left. Follow the hairpin turn away from the waterfall as the road turns into a rocky, unmarked service road; on maps, it's labeled as Baldy Rd.

3. At 0.9 miles, pass a small trail on the left leading uphill. Skip this trail for now but note that you'll come down it at the end of the hike. Continue on Baldy Rd., ignoring the smaller offshoot trails on either side.

4. At 2.5 miles, pass a 15-mph speed limit sign and a chairlift on the right; continue on the switchback going up to the left.

5. At 2.7 miles, pass a small shack on the left and continue on the switchback going right.

6. At 3.2 miles, follow the unmarked switchback heading up to the left, ignoring a trail on the right.

7. At 3.6 miles, reach the Mount Baldy ski resort, including lift access points and the Top of the Notch restaurant; keep slightly left on a small, unmarked trail that heads up under a ski lift. This is the unmarked Devil's Backbone Road.

8. At 3.8 miles, continue straight uphill, ignoring an unmarked trail that doubles back towards a water tower.

9. At 3.9 miles, keep right, heading uphill on the unmarked trail.

10. At 4.3 miles, continue straight uphill, ignoring a trail heading down to the left.

11. At 4.4 miles, keep right at the unmarked fork.

12. At 4.5 miles, pass another lift on the left and continue up to the right, ignoring a trail heading down to the left.

13. At 4.7 miles, reach a sign for the Devil's Backbone Trail and follow this trail along the ridgeline. Ignore any offshoots going off the clearly defined trail.

14. At 5.6 miles, reach a fork in the trail. The right fork leads to Mt. Hardwood, an optional peak that adds approximately 200 feet of elevation gain and 0.2 miles to the route. For our route, take the trail on the left for the most direct path to Mt. Baldy, skipping Mt. Hardwood.

15. At 6.0 miles, the trail from Mt. Hardwood converges with the main trail; continue uphill, starting up a very steep and exposed set of switchbacks.

16. At 6.6 miles, reach the summit of Mt. San Antonio/Mt. Baldy. Take the Baldy Bowl Trail heading down from the summit and to the left towards Manker Camp/Flat.

17. At 7.2 miles, continue straight on the Baldy Bowl Trail towards Manker Camp/Flat, ignoring a set of switchbacks heading downhill to the right.

18. At 7.4 miles, reach a web of small, diverging trails. These all head downhill and lead to the same endpoint in around the same distance; stay on the leftmost trail.

19. At 8.4 miles, cross a small seasonal creek and then keep right, heading downhill and passing a ski hut on the left.

20. At 10.0 miles, emerge onto Baldy Rd. (see Step 3) and turn right to head back to the trailhead.

FIND THE TRAILHEAD

From central Claremont, head north on N Indian Hill Blvd. After 1.7 miles, turn right onto W Baseline Rd. After 0.7 miles, turn left onto N Mills Ave.; proceed for 1.2 miles and then veer right onto Mt. Baldy Rd. Continue on Mt. Baldy Rd. as it winds up the mountain into Angeles National Forest. After 12.4 miles, make a U-turn at an intersection with Falls Rd. The trail begins heading up Falls Rd., but you'll find parking on either side of Mt. Baldy Rd.

CLAREMONT CRAFT ALES

Simon Brown, his wife Emily Moulultrie, Emily's first cousin Natalie Seffer, and Natalie's husband Brian Seffer opened Claremont Craft Ales together in 2012. Previously an engineer and a chef, Simon developed a passion for brewing in 2009 because it was a nice blend of his two former careers. After almost two years of planning, the two couples opened the first and only brewery in Claremont. Over the past eleven years, the brewery has won four Great American Beer Festival gold medals and several other international and local beer competition awards.

Longtime Claremont residents themselves, the brewers champion their community by naming many of their beers after popular local destinations. One of these beers is the refreshing Baldy American Pilsner, which features hops from the Pacific Northwest that provide faint citrus notes along with classic pilsner lightness.

LAND MANAGER

Angeles National Forest
701 N. Santa Anita Ave.
Arcadia, CA 91006
(626) 574-1613
www.fs.usda.gov/angeles
Map: www.fs.usda.gov/detail/angeles/maps-pubs/?cid=FSEPRD631156

BREWERY/RESTAURANT

Claremont Craft Ales
1420 N Claremont Blvd #204c
Claremont, CA 91711
(909) 625-5350
www.claremontcraftales.com/

Distance from trailhead: 14.3 miles

WRIGHT MOUNTAIN

HIKE ALONG THE PACIFIC CREST TRAIL TO MOUNTAIN VIEWS

WRIGHTWOOD

▷⋯ STARTING POINT	⋯✕ DESTINATION
ACORN DRIVE	**WRIGHT MOUNTAIN**
🍺 BREWERY	HIKE TYPE
WRIGHTWOOD BREW COMPANY	**STRENUOUS**
🐾 DOG FRIENDLY	SEASON
YES	**APRIL–SEPTEMBER**
$ FEES	🕐 DURATION
SUGGESTED DONATION	**4 HOURS 25 MIN.**
⌖ MAP REFERENCE	↦ LENGTH
ANGELES NATIONAL FOREST	**7.8 MILES** (ROUND TRIP)
🔍 HIGHLIGHTS	〰 ELEVATION GAIN
MOUNTAIN VIEWS, PINE FORESTS	**2,329 FEET**

HAZY IPA

6.1 % ALCOHOL CONTENT

 HAZY SUNFLOWER

FRUITY, CITRUS

JUICY, FULL-BODIED

BITTERNESS

SWEETNESS

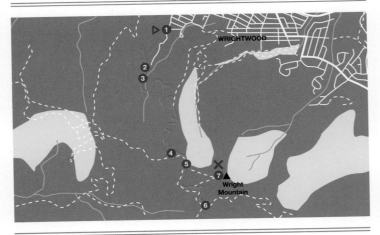

WRIGHTWOOD

Wright Mountain

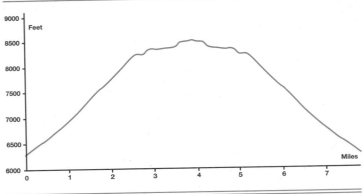

HIKE DESCRIPTION

Enjoy this peaceful yet challenging hike along the PCT through a Jeffrey pine forest. Afterwards, head into town for a tasty sub and a juicy hazy IPA.

This leg-burner of a hike is a favorite local workout on which the journey is the biggest reward. The summit of Wright Mountain doesn't offer a dramatic vista, but the views of surrounding mountains along the way easily make up for this, and on warmer days you'll be glad for the shady tree coverage.

The route begins from a small parking area on Acorn Dr. just before the road becomes private—don't park past this point. At the end of the private residential section of Acorn Dr., the Acorn Trail begins on a dirt fire road, leaving the houses behind. The trail narrows to a singletrack

path soon after you pass a welcome sign for PCT hikers. Wrightwood is a popular stop for thru-hikers on the PCT, who at this point will have walked 360 miles from the Mexican border.

The well-maintained Acorn Trail winds its way up steep switchbacks through Jeffrey pines and other conifers for about two miles to a ridgeline where it intersects with the PCT. In the spring, you'll find a variety of wildflowers like lupine, Indian paintbrush, and western wallflower lining the trail.

At the intersection with the PCT, there's a bench and an excellent view of the rocky ridgeline leading to Pine Mountain. After around half a mile of level hiking on the PCT, you'll pass a memorial for Jodi and Jerry, who died in 1983 along this section of the trail attempting a thru-hike in winter—a feat that wasn't attempted again until 2015.

Shortly after passing a small clearing filled with lupine, Indian paintbrush, and golden yarrow, you'll come upon a faint trail on the left leading up to Wright Mountain. This trail is easy to miss, and the rest of the trail up to the summit isn't particularly well-established either, so downloading the route on your phone ahead of time is essential. The peak is marked with a small pyramid of rocks and a rusted pole with a triangle on top. For an open vista, head just north of the marked summit for a cliffside view overlooking Wrightwood.

TURN-BY-TURN DIRECTIONS

1.   From the parking area, hike up the private part of Acorn Dr.
2.   At 0.5 miles, reach the start of the Acorn Trail; proceed on the Acorn Trail towards the Pacific Crest Trail.
3.   At 0.6 miles, pass a gated-off water tank on the left.
4.   At 2.6 miles, reach the intersection with the Pacific Crest Trail, marked with a sign and a wooden bench. Turn left onto the Pacific Crest Trail towards Highway 15.
5.   At 2.8 miles, pass the memorial plaque for Jodi and Jerry. Keep right on the main trail, hiking parallel to a truck trail.
6.   At 3.5 miles, at a slight left curve, take the faint unmarked trail uphill. Continue following this faint trail to the peak—this may require some GPS navigation.
7.   At 3.9 miles, reach the summit, which is marked with a pile of rocks and a metal pole topped by a triangle. Return the way you came.

FIND THE TRAILHEAD

From Wrightwood Brew Co., head northwest on Irene St. At the end of the block, turn left onto Pine St.; proceed for 0.3 miles, at which point the road turns into Twin Lakes Rd. After 0.1 miles on Twin Lakes Rd., turn right onto Finch Rd. After 0.1 miles, Finch Rd. ends at a T-junction with Acorn Dr.; a parking area with around five spots is on the opposite side of Acorn Dr. If all the spots are taken, you can either look for street parking on the public part of Acorn Dr. or park around Wrightwood Brew Co. and walk the extra 0.6 miles.

WRIGHTWOOD BREW CO.

Kenneth (Ken) Beaujean and Todd Grijalva opened their brewery on 16 August 2016—the same day the Blue Cut wildfire started in the Cajon Pass, less than twenty miles away. The pair wanted to keep the brewery open but had to evacuate the next day. The fire burned 37,000 acres and destroyed 105 homes but didn't make it all the way to the brewery, so Ken and Todd were able to reopen once the fire had been contained. Now, the brewery pays tribute to the fire with its popular Blue Cut IPA, which is brewed once a year.

The Hazy IPA, made with citra mosaic hops, is one of the brewery's staples. Along with the drink, grab a sandwich or two—the recipes come from Ken's mom, who started a sandwich shop in 1986 in Riverside catering to UC Riverside students. The Wrightwood Philly Steak is delicious!

LAND MANAGER

Angeles National Forest
701 N. Santa Anita Ave.
Arcadia, CA 91006
(626) 574-1613
www.fs.usda.gov/angeles
Map: www.fs.usda.gov/detail/angeles/maps-pubs/?cid=FSEPRD631156

BREWERY/RESTAURANT

Wrightwood Brew Co.
1257 Apple Avenue.
Wrightwood, CA. 92397
(760) 488-3163
www.wwbrewco.com/

Distance from trailhead: 0.6 miles

GRAND VIEW POINT

HIKE THROUGH CONIFEROUS FORESTS TO A TRULY GRAND VIEW

BIG BEAR LAKE

▷⋯ STARTING POINT	⋯✕ DESTINATION
ASPEN GLEN PICNIC AREA	**GRAND VIEW POINT**
🍺 BREWERY	HIKE TYPE
BIG BEAR LAKE BREWING COMPANY	**MODERATE**
🐾 DOG FRIENDLY	📅 SEASON
YES (LEASH REQUIRED)	**MAY—OCTOBER**
$ FEES	🕐 DURATION
YES (AMERICA THE BEAUTIFUL)	**3 HOURS 20 MIN.**
🗺 MAP REFERENCE	↦ LENGTH
POSTED AT TRAILHEAD	**8.0 MILES** (ROUND TRIP)
🔍 HIGHLIGHTS	〰 ELEVATION GAIN
MOUNTAIN VIEWS, WILDFLOWERS, LAKE VIEWS	**1,178 FEET**

 8.8 % ALCOHOL CONTENT

SIDEWINDER RED ALE

 AMBER

 MALTY, PINE

 MALTY, FULL-BODY

BITTERNESS

SWEETNESS

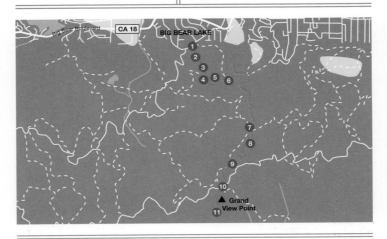

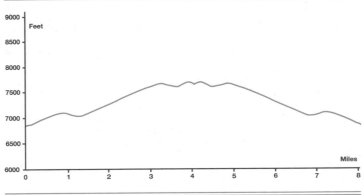

HIKE DESCRIPTION

Hike among conifers and granite boulders to a lofty summit looking out to the San Bernardino Mountains. Afterwards, head back into town to indulge in a malty red ale and heavenly avocado bomb at Big Bear Lake Brewing Co.

At 7,784 feet above sea level, Grand View Point offers views of Big Bear Lake to the north and some of the highest mountains in Southern California, including Anderson Peak and San Gorgonio Peak, to the south. Along the trail you'll probably see ground squirrels and chipmunks, but deer, cottontail bunnies, and coyotes are also regular sightings. There are black bears in this area too, so be aware.

From the Aspen Glen Picnic Area parking lot, you'll follow the clearly marked Pine Knot Trail. Once you pass the official San Bernardino National Forest sign marking the Pine Knot trailhead, the trail splits into many smaller unmarked paths, but as long as you continue uphill in a general southern direction, you'll be going the right way. This is a place where having a map on your phone will help!

Once the various paths merge into a single trail again, you'll climb up steep switchbacks until the end of the first mile, at which point you'll get glimpses of Big Bear Lake from between pine trees. You'll get a quarter-mile break from climbing here, weaving along a forested singletrack trail, and then continue gradually uphill for the next two miles. The elevation gain is noticeable, but you're mostly under shade coverage and the trail is varied enough not to feel like a slog.

Around two miles in, you'll reach a small creek on the right and granite boulders on the left. Another half mile down this forested path, you'll pass several clearings filled with vibrant ferns, corn lilies, and broad-leaf lupine. Soon after these meadows, you'll reach Deer Group Campground on the left—a car-accessible wooded area large enough to host approximately forty tents. Past the campground, you'll hike by another set of granite boulders.

The final stretch to the summit rises out of the main forest and opens up with shorter manzanita bushes and a few dispersed pines. The trail ends at some granite boulders, a bench, and an interpretive display pointing out the different peaks you'll see before you. Just past this stopping point, you'll find another rock outcrop with more unobstructed views of the mountains. This is a great place to take photos before you turn back.

TURN-BY-TURN DIRECTIONS

1. From the Aspen Glen Picnic Area parking lot, follow the paved trail, passing a large interpretive map, an information bulletin, and a small building on the left. Follow signs for the Pine Knot Trail.

2. At 0.2 miles, the trail becomes less defined. Head slightly right to cross over a small gully and then keep left to stay on the right side of the gully for about 150 feet until the trail curves around to the right. Here you'll keep right on the switchbacks heading uphill.

3. At 0.4 miles, keep left on the signposted Pine Knot Trail.

4. At 0.7 miles, stay on the clearest path switchbacking uphill. Ignore smaller, more direct mountain-bike paths—these cause more erosion.

5. At 0.9 miles, continue straight, ignoring an unmarked mountain-bike trail cutting across the main trail.

6. At 1.2 miles, cross a small creek and then keep right on the Pine Knot Trail towards Grand View Point. Ignore any smaller trail spurs for the next mile and a half.

7. At 2.7 miles, reach the intersection with Knickerbocker Rd. (2N08), with a large map of the South Shore Trail Network on the left. Turn left onto Knickerbocker Rd. and then almost immediately right to stay on the Pine Knot Trail.

8. At 2.9 miles, pass the Deer Group Campground on the left.

9. At 3.4 miles, a wide dirt road will emerge parallel to the trail on the right; continue on the singletrack Pine Knot Trail.

10. At an intersection at 3.7 miles, cross the dirt road and continue straight on the Pine Knot Trail towards Grand View Point.

11. At 4.0 miles, reach Grand View Point. Return the way you came.

FIND THE TRAILHEAD

From downtown Big Bear, head west on E Big Bear Blvd./CA-18 and proceed for 5.2 miles. After passing the Big Bear Lake town center, turn right onto Big Bear Blvd. After 0.5 miles, turn left onto Mill Creek Rd. After 0.4 miles, reach the signposted Aspen Glen Picnic Area parking lot on the left.

BIG BEAR LAKE BREWING COMPANY

Dave Stone and Ron Vandenbroeke opened Big Bear Lake Brewing Company in 2014. Since then, Vandenbroeke has taken over managing the business within the Big Bear Lake–based parent company, Stone Entertainment Group. All the brewery's beer recipes come from Vandenbroeke, who has over thirty years of brewing experience.

The Sidewinder red ale is a fan favorite at the brewery. It has a malty, full-body flavor with a hint of piney hops, making it a great brew to have with food or on its own. While the beers are great, the brewery is perhaps best known for its signature avocado bomb: a honey ale–battered half avocado stuffed with spicy ahi and crab shrimp cake.

LAND MANAGER

San Bernardino National Forest
Big Bear Discovery Center
40917 North Shore Dr., Highway 38
Fawnskin, CA 92333
(909) 382-2790
www.fs.usda.gov/detail/sbnf/about-forest/districts/?cid=fsbdev7_007796
Map: www.fs.usda.gov/Internet/FSE_DOCUMENTS/stelprdb5438772.pdf

BREWERY/RESTAURANT

Big Bear Lake Brewing Company
40827 Stone Rd.
Big Bear Lake, CA 92315
(909) 878-0283
www.bblbc.com/

Distance from trailhead: 1.3 miles

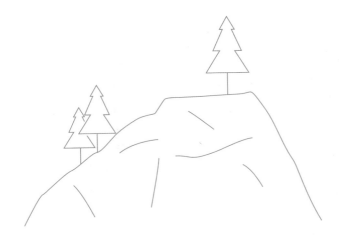

JOSHUA TREE WARREN PEAK

A LESSER-KNOWN CLASSIC IN JOSHUA TREE NATIONAL PARK

JOSHUA TREE

▷⋯ STARTING POINT	⋯✕ DESTINATION
BLACK ROCK CANYON TRAILHEAD	**WARREN PEAK**
🍺 BREWERY	HIKE TYPE
PAPPY AND HARRIET'S/ COACHELLA VALLEY BREWING CO.	**MODERATE**
🐾 DOG FRIENDLY	SEASON
NO	**OCTOBER–APRIL**
$ FEES	⏱ DURATION
YES (AMERICA THE BEAUTIFUL)	**3 HOURS**
⚠ MAP REFERENCE	↦ LENGTH
POSTED AT TRAILHEAD	**5.8 MILES** (ROUND TRIP)
🔍 HIGHLIGHTS	〰 ELEVATION GAIN
JOSHUA TREES, PEAK VIEWS	**1,119 FEET**

DESERT CITRUS WHEAT BEER

GOLDEN

ORANGE, TANGERINE

ORANGE SODA

BITTERNESS

SWEETNESS

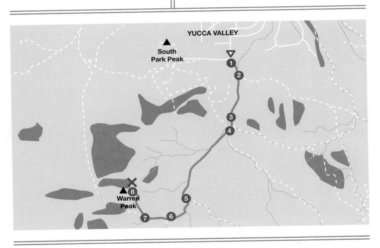

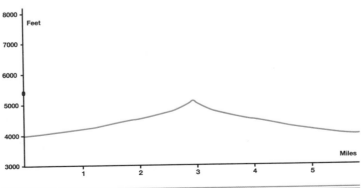

HIKE DESCRIPTION

Head slightly off the beaten path in the iconic Joshua Tree National Park with this excursion up to Warren Peak. Afterwards, head to Pappy and Harriet's, a favorite watering hole in historic Pioneer Town, for a beer from nearby Coachella Valley Brewing Co.

No trip to Southern California is complete without a visit to Joshua Tree National Park. Joshua Tree has approximately 800,000 acres of high desert wilderness to explore, so you'll likely want to plan more than just a day to truly experience it. Known for world-class rock climbing and one of only eight International Dark Sky Parks in the western United States, Joshua Tree has over 300 miles of hiking trails.

The Black Rock area of the park is less frequented than the more popular West Entrance, but it still boasts many of the same features as the other areas, and along the trail to Warren Peak you'll pass through dense forests of Joshua trees (described further in the Wind Turbines PCT Segment hike). These prickly iconic Southern California plants (and the national park's namesake) are only found in this part of the world, from the San Bernardino mountains to the Sonoran Desert in western Arizona, though they are most common in the Mojave Desert. They are not actually trees at all but are instead part of the agave family.

Starting from the Black Rock Campground, you'll set out on the sandy Black Rock Canyon Trail through a Joshua-tree forest. Various other underbrush plants line the trail, including desert willow and silver cholla cactus. The sandy trail starts out relatively flat with just a mild incline, though it can still feel challenging because of how loose the sand is—it's like walking on the dry part of a beach!

Further along the main trail, the sand starts to firm up and get more manageable, though the steepness of the trail also starts to increase. With small hills to either side of the trail, it feels like you're walking along a dry riverbed. Lining the trail and up the hillsides a little past a half-mile in, you'll notice Muller's oak and singleleaf pinyon trees dispersed among the Joshua trees.

The trail leads through a small canyon with striking rock formations as it continues to gradually head uphill. Around two and a half miles in, you'll turn right and see Warren Peak rising directly ahead of you. In that same line of sight, a large Joshua tree stands next to the trail, flaunting a full, bushy set of branches. The final half mile to the peak is brutal, a climb of nearly 400 feet while fully exposed to the sun.

Once at the summit, however, you'll be rewarded with panoramic views of the park's undulating hills and the often-snow-capped San Gorgonio Mountain and San Jacinto Peak to the west.

TURN-BY-TURN DIRECTIONS

1. From the small parking area just outside Black Rock Campground, head down the clear hiking trail marked with a sign for Black Rock Canyon.
2. At 0.2 miles, keep right following the sign-posted arrow towards the Burnt Hill Trail. Stay on the main trail, ignoring smaller, unmarked offshoot trails.
3. At a fork at 0.7 miles, keep right, ignoring the Short Loop Trail on the left.
4. At 0.8 miles, continue straight on the Black Rock Canyon Trail towards Panorama Loop/Warren Peak.
5. At 1.8 miles, reach a sign for the Panorama Loop/Morongo View Trail. Just past this, you'll find a wooden post with a faded arrow and "WP" for Warren Peak. Keep right towards Warren Peak.
6. At 2.2 miles, keep right at the fork for the marked "WP" trail.
7. At 2.5 miles, keep right at an unmarked fork.
8. At 2.9 miles, reach Warren Peak. Return the way you came.

FIND THE TRAILHEAD

From Joshua Tree National Park Visitor Center, head north on Park Blvd. After about 400 feet, turn left onto CA-62/29 Palms Hwy.; proceed for 4.1 miles and then turn left onto Avalon Ave. After 0.7 miles, continue straight onto Palomar Ave. and proceed for another 2.2 miles. At Joshua Ln., turn left. After 0.9 miles, turn right onto San Marino Dr., which almost immediately turns left and becomes Black Rock Canyon Rd. After 0.3 miles, enter the park; keep left to stay on Black Rock Canyon Rd. Around 300 feet down the road, make a U-turn through the gravel median and the primary parking will be on the right. There is additional parking further into the campground at the Black Rock Nature Center.

PAPPY AND HARRIET'S/COACHELLA VALLEY BREWING CO.

The brewery scene around Joshua Tree National Park is complicated by various regulations and challenges specific to the desert, so there hasn't always been a reliably open brewery in the area. However, Joshua Tree is too iconic not to feature in a book on Southern California, which is why this is the only beer hike that slightly bends the book's premise of specifically featuring breweries—but don't worry, you're still getting delightful craft beer. The popular restaurant and live-music venue Pappy and Harriet's has been around since 1982 and serves up a trifecta of canned brews from Coachella Valley Brewing Co. along with an array of classic BBQ foods and small bites. Coachella Valley Brewing Co., based in Thousand Palms just over 40 miles from Joshua Tree, was founded in 2013 with an emphasis on sustainable, farm-to-table brewing and the unique Southern California desert environment.

Served with an orange slice, the desert citrus wheat beer is made with pureed tangerines. The sweet, tangy brew is reminiscent of orange soda and delightfully refreshing on a hot day.

LAND MANAGER

Joshua Tree National Park
74485 National Park Drive
Twentynine Palms, CA 92277-3597
(760) 367-5500
www.nps.gov/jotr/index.htm
Map: www.nps.gov/jotr/planyourvisit/black-rock-area-hiking.htm

BREWERY/RESTAURANT

Pappy and Harriet's
53688 Pioneertown Road
Pioneertown, CA 92268
(760) 228-2222
www.pappyandharriets.com/home/

Coachella Valley Brewing Company
30640 Gunther St.
Thousand Palms, CA 92276
(760 343-5973
www.cvbco.com/

Distance from trailhead: 10.4 miles

RIVERSIDE

MURRAY CANYON

HIKE THROUGH A SECLUDED DESERT OASIS TO CASCADING WATERFALLS.

PALM SPRINGS

▷⋯ STARTING POINT	⋯✕ DESTINATION
ANDREAS CANYON TRAILHEAD	**SEVEN SISTERS WATERFALL**
🍺 BREWERY	🎲 HIKE TYPE
LAS PALMAS	**MODERATE** 🚶
🐾 DOG FRIENDLY	📅 SEASON
NO	**NOVEMBER—MAY**
$ FEES	⏱ DURATION
YES	**3 HOURS**
⛰ MAP REFERENCE	↦ LENGTH
POSTED AT TRAILHEAD	**4.2 MILES** (ROUND TRIP)
🔍 HIGHLIGHTS	〰 ELEVATION GAIN
WATERFALL, WILDFLOWERS	**600 FEET**

TABLE PETITE
FARMHOUSE ALE

 STRAW

CITRUS

STRAW,
LIGHT

BITTERNESS   SWEETNESS

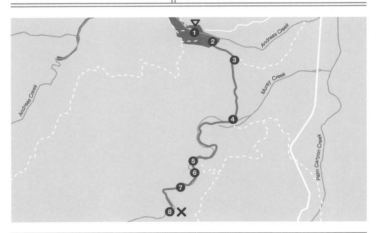

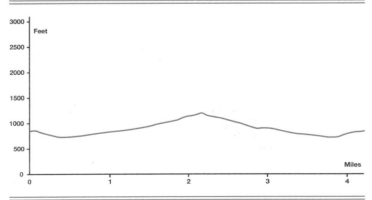

HIKE DESCRIPTION

Hike through the desert and traverse hidden Murray Canyon to reach an enchanting waterfall. Then head to downtown Palm Springs and cool down with a farmhouse ale at the family-owned Las Palmas brewery.

The Murray Canyon Trail goes through Indian Canyons, a nature preserve that's part of the Agua Caliente Indian Reservation and is managed by the Agua Caliente Band of Cahuilla Indians. This band lived in the Palm Springs area well before any pioneers or European settlers. Today, the Agua Caliente area spans approximately 31,000 acres of reservation and 7,000 acres of off-reservation land stretching across Riverside County and the cities of Palm Springs, Cathedral City, and Rancho Mirage. For further information about the Agua Caliente Band of Cahuilla Indians, stop by the Trading Post—a small shop by Palm Canyon with unique souvenirs, cultural information, and regular ranger-led hikes and talks.

While neighboring Palm Canyon often steals the limelight as the world's largest oasis of California fan palms, Murray Canyon offers a more under-the-radar beauty, with a bubbling creek in the winter and spring, vibrant desert flowers in the spring, and plenty of the majestic fan palms. Shaded by palms, you'll set out from the Andreas Canyon trailhead on a wide dirt road, walk through a palm oasis picnic area, and then reach the official start of the Murray Canyon Trail. From here, you'll venture about half a mile into a more exposed desert landscape. In the spring, this dry desert comes alive with blankets of brittlebush, desert lavender, and Canterbury bells.

Just under a mile in, you'll spot a clear line of California fan palms ahead— these line Murray Creek, which the trail leads to. The California fan palm is the only palm tree native to California and is an iconic fixture in the Coachella Valley. The Cahuilla people used the palms to build shelters called kish and craft hunting bows and eating utensils. A Cahuilla legend says that the first palm was a Cahuilla leader who sacrificed himself and transformed into the fruiting palm tree to provide for his people.

Once the trail converges with the creek, the rest of the hike sticks close to the water and crosses it at least ten times each way. Depending on the water level, these crossings can be easy and dry rock jumps or

more technical river crossings that involve wading through knee-high water. The trail ends at the base of the tiered Seven Sisters waterfall. From the official end of the trail, you can access the smaller, segmented, cascade-like waterfall, and, if you're comfortable scrambling, you can climb up some rock on the right of the falls to reach the taller, single-point falls above.

TURN-BY-TURN DIRECTIONS

1. From the Andreas Canyon Trailhead parking, cross a flat bridge with metal railings. Continue straight on a wide dirt road towards the Murray Canyon Trail. Stay on the road as it curves to the left past some picnic tables and additional parking.

2. At 0.2 miles, you'll find the official start of the Murray Canyon Trail marked with a large map and information about Indian Canyons.

3. At 0.4 miles, keep right on the Murray Canyon Trail.

4. At 0.8 miles, cross Murray Creek. Then keep right on the Murray Canyon Trail. The trail stays close to the creek from here and is generally easy to follow, clearly emerging on the other side after each creek crossing.

5. At 1.5 miles, continue straight on the Murray Canyon Trail, ignoring trails on either side around 100 feet apart from each other.

6. At 1.6 miles, pass a "No Horses, Hiking Only" signpost and cross the creek again.

7. After a river crossing at 1.8 miles, the trail makes a steeper, slightly more challenging ascent up rocks on the left side of the creek. This is easily manageable but requires a bit more thought about foot and hand placements.

8. At 2.2 miles, reach the end of the trail and the base of the Seven Sisters Falls. Return the way you came.

FIND THE TRAILHEAD

From Palm Springs, head south on N Palm Canyon Dr. After 2.0 miles, veer right onto S Palm Canyon Dr. Proceed for 2.8 miles until you reach the Indian Canyon Entrance, where you'll pay the entrance fee and continue for another 0.1 miles. At the next fork in the road, turn right in the direction of Andreas Canyon Trailhead (posted sign). Continue on this road until it ends at trailhead parking on both sides. There is additional parking across the bridge.

LAS PALMAS BREWING

This unassuming little taproom, two-barrel production microbrewery, and natural wine bar opened in October 2019. Owners Rey Romero and Sam Gill had been working at a brewery in San Francisco when they met, but Romero is originally from the Palm Springs area and Gill from LA. They were intrigued that there was no production brewery in Palm Springs and decided they'd be the first.

The brewery specializes in creating all-natural beers without additives, chemicals, filtration, or fining. Beers are brewed at ambient temperatures. Gill, the head brewer, works around summer temperatures that head into the triple digits by brewing early in the morning and using primarily Kveik yeast, which thrives in warmer climates. Given the sweltering temperatures, Las Palmas specializes in light, crushable beers like the Table Farmhouse Ale, which is dry and refreshing with subtle hints of citrus and straw. Las Palmas hosts a variety of pop-up food vendors in the beer garden and a chess club that meets on the last day of each month.

LAND MANAGER

Agua Caliente Band of Cahuilla Indians
5401 Dinah Shore Drive
Palm Springs, CA 92264
(760) 699-6800
www.indian-canyons.com/indian_canyons
Map: www.acbci.maps.arcgis.com/apps/View/index.html?appid=1309d967735d4c4897115848d0056f0f

BREWERY/RESTAURANT

Las Palmas Brewing
461 N Palm Canyon Dr.
Palm Springs, CA 92262
(760) 992-5082
www.laspalmasbrewing.com/

Distance from trailhead: 5.8 miles

SUICIDE ROCK

A FORESTED HIKE TO A STUNNING GRANITE OUTCROP

IDYLLWILD-PINE COVE

▷⋯ STARTING POINT	⋯✗ DESTINATION
DEER SPRINGS TRAILHEAD	**SUICIDE ROCK**
◻ BREWERY	▦ HIKE TYPE
IDYLLWILD BREWPUB	**MODERATE** 🚶
🐾 DOG FRIENDLY	📅 SEASON
NO	**MAY–NOVEMBER**
$ FEES	🕐 DURATION
NONE (FREE PERMIT REQUIRED)	**3 HOURS 40 MIN.**
⚠ MAP REFERENCE	↦ LENGTH
MOUNT SAN JACINTO STATE PARK BROCHURE	**7.3 MILES** (ROUND TRIP)
🔍 HIGHLIGHTS	〰 ELEVATION GAIN
SUMMIT VIEWS, WATERFALL, WILDFLOWERS	**1,929 FT**

 5.1 %
ALCOHOL CONTENT

LONE WILLOW DARK LAGER

 BLACK-BROWN

 MALTY, COFFEE

 LIGHT, CHOCOLATE

BITTERNESS   **SWEETNESS**

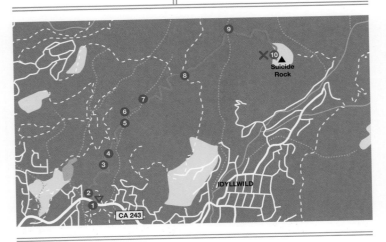

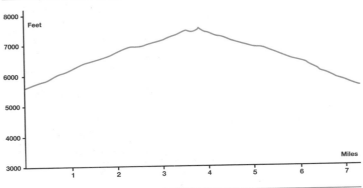

HIKE DESCRIPTION

Follow this forested trail past a small waterfall to far-reaching views of the San Jacinto mountains and Tahquitz Rock. Posthike, head into the mountain town of Idyllwild and grab a brew and burger from the local treehouse-like brewpub.

Officially part of San Bernardino National Forest, Suicide Rock reaches an elevation of 7,528 feet and is one of the most popular hikes around Idyllwild. Legend has it that a Native American princess and her lover chose suicide by jumping off the rock rather than let tribal or parental restrictions keep them apart. The *Idyllwild Town Crier*, however, notes that this legend may have been invented to increase tourism in the early 1900s.

Our route follows the Deer Springs Trail, which begins and ends in the San Bernardino National Forest but goes through Mount Jacinto State Park and Wilderness. Its 1,929 feet of elevation gain will make you feel like you've worked for the views, but it's not so steep that it's a suffer-fest. The trail requires a free day-use permit from either the state park or national forest; you can get these from 24-hour kiosks at the Idyllwild Forest Service Ranger Station or the state park headquarters in Idyllwild.

From the parking area off Hwy. 243, the trail heads uphill between man-zanita bushes. The first mile and a half also provides dappled shade coverage from pine and oak trees. As the trail climbs into higher eleva-tions, the manzanita gives way to more pine and oak trees, with wild-flowers including lupin, Indian paintbrush, and snow plant in the understory. The snow plant sprouts as a single, 6- to 12-inch fluores-cent scarlet stalk of flowers and has no leaves or stem. This is because it doesn't photosynthesize but instead feeds off a fungus in the roots of conifer trees.

A little past the two-mile mark, you'll reach a path diverging off the Deer Springs Trail and heading towards Suicide Rock. Around a half mile further along, you'll cross a creek with a small set of falls. The trail continues gradually uphill until the rocky vista point of Suicide Rock, where you'll enjoy a full view looking down on Idyllwild and towards the large granite outcrop of Tahquitz Rock across the valley. This flat sec-tion is the end of the designated trail; to get to the actual peak, you can scramble the last hundred feet to an unassuming summit with a few boulders around it.

TURN-BY-TURN DIRECTIONS

1. From the parking area, head up the hill away from the road on a sandy unmarked trail through manzanita bushes.

2. At 0.1 miles, join a wide unmarked dirt road; keep left. 200 feet up the road, reach a sign for the Mount San Jacinto State Park Deer Springs Trail that reiterates the permit requirements; keep right towards the Santa Rosa and San Jacinto Mountains National Monument.

3. At 0.6 miles, pass a sign saying you're entering the State Park Wilderness.

4. At 0.7 miles, keep left to stay on the main trail, ignoring a faint trail heading straight and blocked off by some small rocks.

5. At 1.2 miles, pass a small seasonal creek on the right and keep left, following the challenging switchbacks.

6. At 1.3 miles, keep right and proceed on the rock, ignoring a small blocked-off trail heading straight. Follow the trail uphill along the rock for approximately 150 feet and then to the right of a wall of granite boulders.

7. At 1.5 miles, cross a small creek.

8. At the junction at 2.3 miles, keep right for Suicide Rock.

9. At 2.9 miles, cross a creek with a small, tiered waterfall.

10. At 3.6 miles, come to the end of the trail for Suicide Rock. On the left is the granite outcrop from which you'll see Suicide Rock's famed views. The actual summit is to the right of the official end of the trail; there is no trail leading to it, but you can find your way up the steep hill to the boulders that mark the summit.

FIND THE TRAILHEAD

From the center of San Jacinto, head east on Main St. After 1.2 miles, turn right onto W Ramona Expy. After 3.5 miles, turn left onto E Florida Ave./CA-74, which becomes a windy mountain road. After 14.4 miles, take a slight left towards CA-243, pass a gas station, and then, at the stop sign, turn left onto CA-243 N. Proceed for 5.2 miles on CA-243 N, driving past Idyllwild center. The trailhead parking will be on the right directly after a sign for the Deer Springs Trail and Deer Springs Trailhead Parking.

IDYLLWILD BREWPUB

Idyllwild Brewpub demonstrates its commitment to the outdoors and the local community, both in its appearance and in its practices. Backed by a generous investor, the brewpub team spent four years designing and building the space from the ground up with help from a longtime resident architect and local contractors. The result is a rustic, tree house–like brewery and restaurant that employs high-tech sustainability practices, its own mountain well water, and solar panels. For its efforts, the brewpub won a sustainability award from Riverside County's Department of Waste Resources when it opened in 2017.

Head brewer Don Put has been brewing since 1989 and has been with Idyllwild Brewpub since it opened. The Lone Willow dark lager is a favorite brew regularly on tap that pairs well with a burger or bratwurst. The dark lager features the malt profile of a stout but the light easy-drinking base of a lager.

LAND MANAGER

San Bernardino National Forest
San Jacinto Ranger District
54270 Pine Crest
Idyllwild, CA 92549
(909) 382-2921
www.fs.usda.gov/detail/sbnf/about-forest/districts/?cid=fsbdev7_007800
Map: www.parks.ca.gov/pages/636/files/MtSanJacintoSPFinalWeb-Layout2018.pdf

BREWERY/RESTAURANT

Idyllwild Brewpub
54423 Village Center Dr.
Idyllwild-Pine Cove, CA 92549
(951) 659-0163
www.idyllwildbrewpub.com/

Distance from trailhead: 1.2 miles

WILD HORSE TRAIL

A PEACEFUL CANYON HIKE THROUGH UNTOUCHED WILDERNESS

TEMECULA

▷⋯ STARTING POINT	⋯✕ DESTINATION
DRIPPING SPRINGS CAMPGROUND	**CANYON OVERLOOK**
🍺 BREWERY	HIKE TYPE
8 BIT BREWING COMPANY	**STRENUOUS**
🐾 DOG FRIENDLY	📅 SEASON
YES (LEASH REQUIRED)	**JANUARY—MAY**
$ FEES	🕐 DURATION
YES (AMERICA THE BEAUTIFUL)	**5 HOURS**
⌂ MAP REFERENCE	↦ LENGTH
POSTED AT TRAILHEAD	**11.9 MILES** (ROUND TRIP)
🔎 HIGHLIGHTS	∿ ELEVATION GAIN
MOUNTAIN VIEWS, WILDFLOWERS	**1,991 FEET**

5.1 %
ALCOHOL
CONTENT

GUARDIANS OF
SUNLIGHT LAGER

👁	STRAW
👃	HAY, GRAIN
👅	CRISP, LIGHT

BITTERNESS

5
4
3
2
1

SWEETNESS

5
4
3
2
1

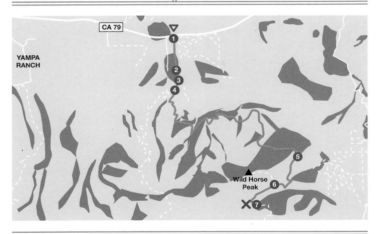

CA 79

YAMPA
RANCH

1
2
3
4
5
Wild Horse
Peak
6
✕ 7

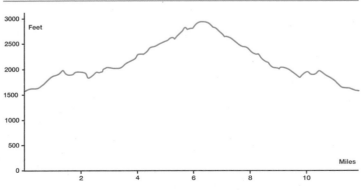

3000
2500
2000
1500
1000
500
0

Feet

Miles

2   4   6   8   10

HIKE DESCRIPTION

Enjoy this charming trail for a full day's hike through canyons in the Agua Tibia Wilderness. Afterwards, head into Murreta for a refreshing brew and rewarding posthike meal from 8 Bit Brewing Company.

The beauty of this hike is that you can make it as long or as short as you want—anywhere from an almost twenty-mile loop to a friendly four-mile out-and-back that still features stunning canyon views.

Our route begins in the Cleveland National Forest, just outside the Dripping Springs Campground. After passing through the campsite, you'll come upon a sign and large map for the trail and then almost immediately reach a seasonal creek. The creek can be wildly different—anything from 15-feet-wide, knee-deep rushing water to completely dry—so be sure to check on recent conditions so you know what to expect. During certain times in the spring and summer the creek closes to everything other than trail access to protect the riparian habitat for the endangered arroyo toad, so watch your feet while crossing and look out for this squat little creature!

Shortly after crossing the creek, you'll enter the Agua Tibia Wilderness and follow the Wild Horse Trail through chaparral with plants including California buckwheat, chamise, and toyon. After the fork of the Wild

Horse Trail and the Dripping Springs Trail, you'll hike the first uphill section, a singletrack trail with several switchbacks. Around a mile and a half in, the trail evens out and reveals impressive views of the canyon below. The next two miles are relatively flat, passing through the canyon among chaparral plants. In the spring, the area will often bloom with a spectacular array of wildflowers including California poppy, monkey flower, and cardinal catchfly.

Around the 3.5-mile mark, the trail begins a gradual but steady climb along the side of the canyon. It can be overgrown and narrow in places, with a steep drop to the left, so step carefully. Around five and a half miles in, the dirt and rock along the trail become a rust-red color, and shortly after this you'll pass a faint unmarked trail heading upward; this rugged, washed-out path leads to Wild Horse Peak. Instead of heading up the peak, you'll continue on the main Wild Horse Trail for another half mile, curving around a small valley and reaching several boulders that make great seating for lunch or a snack. This is our turnaround point, though you can keep going if you want—just remember that you have to get back too!

TURN-BY-TURN DIRECTIONS

1. From the Dripping Springs Trailhead Parking, head down the road and walk through the campground.
2. At 0.4 miles, at the end of the campground, pass through a metal gate; continue on the road to a small turnaround loop and the end of the road. Pass a bulletin with a large map and a trail register and set off on the Agua Tibia Wilderness trail.
3. At 0.5 miles, cross a seasonal creek.
4. At 0.6 miles, veer left onto the Wild Horse Trail.
5. At 4.8 miles, pass a large boulder on the right.
6. At 5.7 miles, reach a faint unmarked trail on the right for Wild Horse Peak; continue straight on the more defined Wild Horse Trail.
7. At 6.3 miles, after a switchback in the trail, reach several boulders on either side of the trail and a small opening in the trees that offers a view down the valley to the left. Turn around and return the way you came.

FIND THE TRAILHEAD

From Old Town Temecula, head southeast on Old Town Front St. After 1.0 miles, turn left onto CA-79 S/Temecula Pkwy. After 10.7 miles, turn right at the Cleveland National Forest sign for Dripping Springs Campground. Directly after the turn, a small parking lot will be on the right.

8 BIT BREWING COMPANY

After homebrewing together for several years, friends Chris Keyson and Lamar Ingram founded 8 Bit Brewing Company with Chris's brother Jeff in 2015. Before starting the brewery, Ingram was a video game designer. The team bonded over a nostalgic love for classic 8-bit video games—hence the name. Since 8 Bit's modest start in a single unit in an industrial warehouse, the brewery has expanded to occupy four units with a full kitchen, arcade, and patio. While the beer is top notch, the food stands on its own as well—fan favorites include the burger and the BBQ pork mac & cheese.

Head brewer Neil Willcoxson has been at 8 Bit for the past five years, working his way up from food runner to various jobs in the brew house to his current position. The light, crushable Guardians of Sunlight lager is the brewery's answer to folks who want Coors Light, but craft. The subtle flavors have just a touch of sweetness and floral character, thanks to the use of rice as a supplementary malt.

LAND MANAGER

Cleveland National Forest
Palomar Ranger District
1634 Black Canyon Rd.
Ramona, CA 92065
(760) 788-0250
www.fs.usda.gov/detail/cleveland/home/?cid=FSEPRD477260
Map: www.blm.gov/visit/agua-tibia-wilderness

BREWERY/RESTAURANT

8 Bit Brewing Company
26755 Jefferson Avenue, Suite F
Murrieta, CA 92562
(951) 677-2322
www.8bitbrewingcompany.com/

Distance from trailhead: 15.3 miles

MOUNT RUBIDOUX

AN ACCESSIBLE HIKE WITH EXPANSIVE VIEWS, A GIANT CROSS, AND A PEACE TOWER

RIVERSIDE

▷⋯ STARTING POINT	⋯✕ DESTINATION
RYAN BONAMINIO PARK PARKING LOT	**MOUNT RUBIDOUX**
🍺 BREWERY	HIKE TYPE
ALL POINTS BREWING COMPANY	**EASY**
🐾 DOG FRIENDLY	SEASON
YES (LEASH REQUIRED)	**YEAR-ROUND**
$ FEES	⊘ DURATION
NONE	**1 HOUR 30 MIN.**
⌂ MAP REFERENCE	↦ LENGTH
MOUNT RUBIDOUX PARKING	**3.4 MILES** (LOLLIPOP LOOP)
👁 HIGHLIGHTS	∿ ELEVATION GAIN
PEACE TOWER, CROSS, SUMMIT VIEWS	**554 FT**

PANORAMIC PORTER

6.0%
ALCOHOL CONTENT

BLACK-BROWN

VANILLA,
CHOCOLATE

MALTY,
VANILLA

BITTERNESS
5
4
3
2
1

SWEETNESS
5
4
3
2
1

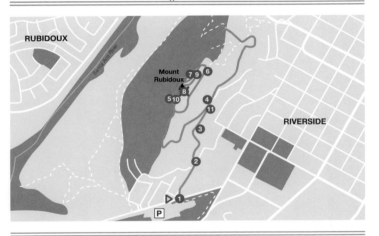

RUBIDOUX

Santa Ana River

Mount
Rubidoux

RIVERSIDE

P

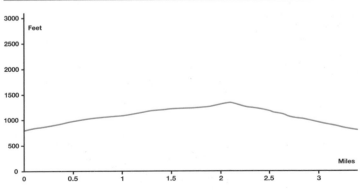

Feet

3000
2500
2000
1500
1000
500
0

0   0.5   1   1.5   2   2.5   3

Miles

HIKE DESCRIPTION

This mostly paved, beginner-friendly hike features impressive panoramic views and a variety of interesting monuments, including a photogenic stone tower and bridge and a large white cross. Posthike, enjoy a delicious vanilla porter in the welcoming atmosphere of All Points Brewing Company.

The Mount Rubidoux Trail in Frank A. Miller Mt. Rubidoux Memorial Park is ideal for people new to hiking, folks who want a quick but rewarding walk, young kids, and anyone with mobility challenges. It's almost fully paved and easy to follow. Yet with 554 feet of elevation gain, it still provides a worthwhile workout and summit views of the surrounding area. The trail is wheelchair- and stroller-friendly most of the way, but wheelchair users will likely need assistance on a few of the steep sections, which have up to a 12% gradient. The final 0.1 miles to the peak includes stairs and some light scrambling and is not wheelchair accessible.

At 1,331 feet, Mount Rubidoux stands out as a high point above Riverside and has become a popular landmark for the area. The park has two primary monuments, both of which you'll see along the trail. The first one is the Peace Tower and Friendship Bridge. Built in 1925 and dedicated to former park owner Frank Miller, the design of the Peace Tower and Friendship Bridge was inspired by a bridge in Alcántara, Spain. At the summit, you'll see the second monument—a large white cross dedicated to Father Junipero Serra, the 18th-century founder of California's colonizing mission system. This is the site of the oldest outdoor non-denominational Easter sunrise service in the United States.

The park does not have a big lot, so it's best to leave your car at the nearby Ryan Bonaminio Park and walk up the street to the official trailhead. The mostly paved trail winds around and up the mountain. While circling up the mountain, you'll get views of the nearby mountain ranges on either side in the San Bernardino National Forest and Angeles National Forest.

TURN-BY-TURN DIRECTIONS

1. Starting at the Ryan Bonaminio Park parking lot, head up the hill on San Andreas Dr.
2. At 0.2 miles, reach the entrance of the park, marked by a sign saying "Welcome to Frank A. Miller Mt. Rubidoux Memorial Park." Turn left into the park and keep left on the paved trail marked with a City of Riverside sign. Stay on the paved path ignoring any side paths.
3. At 0.4 miles, you'll get a first view of the Peace Tower and an American flag higher up the mountain ahead of you.
4. At 0.6 miles, continue straight, crossing 10 feet of sandy path to another switchbacking unmarked paved trail. Keep left, following the trail uphill.
5. At 1.6 miles, walk under the Ben Lewis Bridge and then keep left, continuing uphill.
6. At 1.9 miles, reach the Peace Tower and Friendship Bridge and follow the trail under the bridge.
7. At 2.0 miles, veer left on the unmarked paved path going up to the summit.
8. At 2.1 miles, at the large stone steps, the easiest way to continue is to take the smaller steps on the far right and then scramble up to the summit cross. After enjoying the view, turn back the way you came to the main trail.
9. At 2.2 miles, where the trail forks, turn left and head downhill on the unmarked paved trail.
10. At 2.4 miles, cross over the Ben Lewis Bridge and then keep right, heading downhill on the unmarked paved trail. (The path on the left is the trail you took on the way up.)
11. At 2.9 miles, pass a plaque for Huntington Rock with quotes from the bible and John Muir and then take a sharp right and head back down the path you came up on. From here, continue the way you came to reach the parking lot at Ryan Bonaminio Park.

FIND THE TRAILHEAD

From downtown Riverside, head northwest on University Ave. After 0.2 miles, turn left onto Brockton Ave. and continue for 0.7 miles. Turn right onto Tequesquite Ave. Continue for 0.3 miles and then turn left onto Palm Ave. Take the next right back onto Tequesquite Ave. Stay on Tequesquite Ave for 0.3 miles until you see Ryan Bonaminio Park and the free parking lot (with restrooms) on the left.

ALL POINTS BREWING COMPANY

In March 2021, co-owners and co-brewers Don McAllister and Matt Rose opened All Points Brewing Company. Don has been homebrewing since 1993 and is the founder and former owner of the Riverside-based Packinghouse Brewing Company. All Points is a welcoming and dog-friendly brewery that always has eight beers, two hard seltzers, and two non-alcoholic craft sodas on tap. The brewery regularly hosts live music and open mic nights and works with a variety of food vendors. The Panoramic Porter is one of its core beers. Don originally brewed the vanilla porter as a Mother's Day gift for his wife over fifteen years ago and has been perfecting the recipe ever since.

LAND MANAGER

City of Riverside Parks, Recreation and Community Services
6927 Magnolia Ave.
Riverside, CA 92506
(951) 826-2000
www.riversideca.gov/park_rec/facilities-parks/mt-rubidoux
Map: www.riversideca.gov/sites/default/files/img/Mt.-Rubidoux-Map.jpg

BREWERY/RESTAURANT

All Points Brewing Company
2023 Chicago Ave., Unit B8
Riverside, CA 92507
(951) 213-6258
www.facebook.com/allpointsbrewingcompany

Distance from trailhead: 4.0 miles

ORANGE

SAN JUAN HILL AND TELEGRAPH CANYON

HIKE THROUGH THE LUSH HILLSIDES ABOVE ANAHEIM

YORBA LINDA

▷⋯ STARTING POINT	⋯✕ DESTINATION
RIMCREST TRAILHEAD	**SAN JUAN HILL**
🍺 BREWERY	🗓 HIKE TYPE
STEREO BREWING COMPANY	**MODERATE**
🐾 DOG FRIENDLY	📅 SEASON
NO	**YEAR-ROUND**
$ FEES	🕐 DURATION
NONE	**3 HOURS 20 MIN.**
⛰ MAP REFERENCE	↦ LENGTH
CHINO HILLS STATE PARK BROCHURE	**8.1 MILES** (LOOP)
🔍 HIGHLIGHTS	〰 ELEVATION GAIN
WILDLIFE, MOUNTAIN AND CITY VIEWS	**1,102 FEET**

OATMEAL STOUT

5.6 %
ALCOHOL
CONTENT

WALL OF SOUND STOUT

 PITCH BLACK

 ROASTED COFFEE, CACAO

 ROASTY, MALTY

BITTERNESS

SWEETNESS

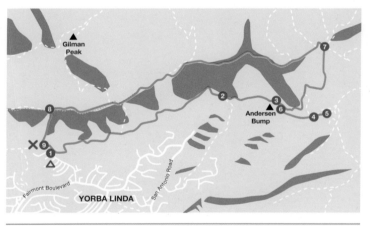

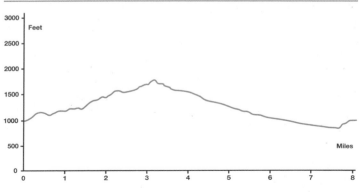

HIKE DESCRIPTION

Drink in the landscape of Chino Hills State Park on this loop through tall grasses and wildflowers. Then enjoy the welcoming vibes and good music at Stereo Brewing over a cold pint.

A vital link in the Puente–Chino Hills Wildlife Corridor, Chino Hills State Park encompasses 14,100 acres of rolling hills and valleys with tall grasses, oaks, sycamores, and many other native species. (See the Whittier Hill hike for more information on wildlife corridors.)

Starting in a residential neighborhood, this loop hike goes along four different popular trails in the park: the South Ridge Trail, the Bovinian Delight Trail, the Telegraph Canyon Trail, and the Easy Street Trail. Starting on the South Ridge Trail, it heads through tall grass on a wide dirt path along a ridge on the border of the park. You're fully exposed to the sun here, so this is not an ideal trail for hot summer days. Our destination is San Juan Hill at around the three-mile mark—at 1,781 feet, this is

the highest point in the park. It offers panoramic views over the Los Angeles basin, the east side of the Chino Hills, and all the way out to the San Gabriel and San Bernardino Mountains to the north and east.

On the back end of the hike, you'll make a gradual descent on a small over-grown trail to Four Corners—a notable trail intersection named to acknowl-edge that the State Park connects the four corners of the counties of Orange, Los Angeles, San Bernardino, and Riverside. Here, you'll find a large interpretive display with information about the park's history, geology, flora, and fauna. You'll then hike on the Telegraph Canyon Trail next to Tele-graph Creek with intermittent shade from oak and walnut trees.

In the spring, you'll see wildflowers covering the hillsides. But when the heat cranks up in summer and early fall, keep an eye out for another excit-ing show of nature: tarantula mating season. The male tarantulas will be out and about, wandering the trails looking for a female's burrow. While tarantulas are usually nocturnal and don't often leave their burrows, during mating season the males can travel up to four miles from their home base. The typical mating season runs from August to October, but it can start as early as June and last until November. Tarantulas get a bad rap as creepy and dangerous animals, but are actually fairly docile, move slowly, and only bite when especially threatened. (And the bite is typically more like a bee sting than anything causing serious harm.)

TURN-BY-TURN DIRECTIONS

1. Head away from the road on the only wide dirt trail and come to a metal gate blocking motor traffic. Cross through the pedestrian gateway and immediately come to a four-way intersection; turn right on the South Ridge Trail towards San Juan Hill and Rolling M Ranch. Stay on the obvious wide trail and ignore any smaller trails on either side.
2. At 2.1 miles, reach a fork in the trail and keep left on the South Ridge Trail.
3. At 2.7 miles, pass the Bovinian Delight Trail on the left. For now, ignore it and continue straight, but take note of this trail because you'll take it coming back from San Juan Hill.
4. At 3.1 miles, veer right onto a small, overgrown trail signed for San Juan Hill.
5. At 3.2 miles, reach the summit of San Juan Hill. Turn around and return to the Bovinian Delight Trail.
6. At 3.7 miles, turn right on the Bovinian Delight Trail.
7. At 4.7 miles, reach Four Corners with its interpretive display, shaded picnic tables, and bathroom. Turn left on the Telegraph Canyon Trail. Ignore all other smaller trails and stay on the Telegraph Canyon Trail.
8. At 7.6 miles, turn left onto the Easy Street Trail.
9. At 8.0 miles, reach the end of the loop and continue straight back to the road.

FIND THE TRAILHEAD

From Central Anaheim, head east on Lincoln Ave. After 0.7 miles, turn left onto N East St. After 1.1 miles, turn right to merge onto CA-91 E towards Riverside; proceed for 6.9 miles. Take the exit on the right for Imperial Hwy/CA-90. At the end of the off-ramp, turn left onto Imperial Hwy. After 1.6 miles, take the exit on the right for Kellogg Dr. At the end of the off-ramp, turn right onto Kellogg Dr.; continue for 1.1 miles until the road ends at Yorba Linda Blvd., where you'll turn right. After 0.3 miles, turn left onto Fairmont Blvd. After 1.6 miles, turn left onto Rimcrest Dr. The trailhead will be on your right in 0.4 miles at a left turn just before the first house, where the road turns into Blue Gum Dr.

The only public parking is along the right side of Rim Crest Dr. before you reach the trailhead. Parking on any side streets or on Blue Gum Dr. is for residents only.

STEREO BREWING COMPANY

Owners Amanda and Rick Smets met at a Bob Dylan concert in 2010 while waiting in line for a craft brew and fell in love over music and beer. Rick was already a professional brewer, while Amanda loved craft beer and had a wide range of work experience. The couple decided to create their own brewery blending good music, balanced beer, and friendly vibes, and in 2016, Stereo Brewing opened its doors. Since then, the brewery has won five Great American Beer Festival medals and a host of other awards and cultivated a fun, welcoming space for regulars and visitors alike to hang out in, meet new people, and drink beer.

The brewery hosts local food trucks, which are announced on its website. The two-time GABF-winning Wall of Sound oatmeal stout is named after the Grateful Dead's touring sound system in the summer of '74. The pitch-black brew features big roasted malt flavors while the dry finish and lower ABV make it especially refreshing.

LAND MANAGER

Chino Hills State Park
4721 Sapphire Road
Chino Hills, CA 91709
(951) 780-6222
www.parks.ca.gov/?page_id=648
Map: www.parks.ca.gov/pages/648/files/ChinoHillsFinalWeb
Layout2018.pdf

BREWERY/RESTAURANT

Stereo Brewing Company
950 S Vía Rodeo
Placentia, CA 92870
(714) 993-3390
www.stereobrewing.com/

Distance from trailhead: 5.3 miles

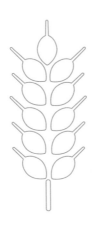

WEIR CANYON

MARVEL AT SPRING WILDFLOWER BLOOMS

ANAHEIM

▷··· STARTING POINT	···✗ DESTINATION
S. HIDDEN CANYON RD.	**POPPY FIELDS**
🍺 BREWERY	HIKE TYPE
GREEN CHEEK BEER COMPANY	**EASY**
🐾 DOG FRIENDLY	📅 SEASON
YES (LEASH REQUIRED)	**FEBRUARY–APRIL**
$ FEES	🕐 DURATION
NONE	**1 HOUR 30 MIN.**
⛰ MAP REFERENCE	↦ LENGTH
SANTIAGO OAKS REGIONAL PARK (POSTED AT TRAILHEAD)	**3.8 MILES** (LOLLIPOP LOOP)
🔍 HIGHLIGHTS	〰 ELEVATION GAIN
WILDFLOWERS	**640 FEET**

DDH RADIANT BEAUTY IPA

 GOLD

 HOPPY, PINE

 DRY, EARTHY

BITTERNESS   **SWEETNESS**

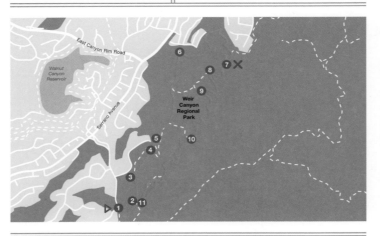

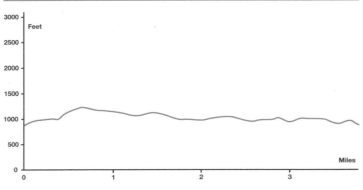

HIKE DESCRIPTION

Meander through fields of vibrant wildflowers on this mild hike through rolling hills. Afterwards, head over to the small independent Green Cheek Beer Co. for a classic West Coast IPA.

While Weir Canyon is open year-round, it transforms from dry desert hillsides to lush green pastures full of colorful wildflowers in the spring. Entire hillsides turn golden-orange from California poppies, with other colors sprinkled in from wild mustard, lupine, Parry's phacelia, forget-me-not, and Indian paintbrush. During especially wet years, this area can explode in color in a "superbloom"—a rare desert botanical phenomenon in which wildflower seeds that have been dormant for years all bloom at once after heavy rains.

In 2019, extensive rainfall in Southern California caused an especially breathtaking superbloom in Walker Canyon in neighboring Riverside county. Excited visitors overwhelmed the area, leading to the closure of Walker Canyon to visitors during wildflower season. It's particularly

important to be respectful of this area to avoid further closures. Don't walk off the trail, and keep your dog on the trail as well. Go early and if the parking is full when you arrive, accept a longer walk-in or opt for a different hike (don't park illegally). Follow leave-no-trace practices.

After a gradual climb on a narrow packed-dirt trail cutting through green grass and small wildflower clusters, you'll head up a steep singletrack path lined with waist-high wild mustard flowers. Though it is beautiful, wild mustard—also known as black mustard—is an invasive species. Originally from Southern Europe and the Middle East, it became part of the California wildflower landscape when Spanish colonizers brought it over and (so the story goes) intentionally planted it along the roads connecting their missions to symbolically mark the way between them. Today it outcompetes many native species and negatively impacts ecosystems, decreasing biodiversity and creating fodder for summer wildfires.

After passing through the wild-mustard flowers, you'll merge onto a wider sandy path that levels out and offers an expansive view over Walnut Canyon Reservoir and the suburban area of Anaheim Hills. Descending on a wide path, you'll wind between hillsides and start to see more and more clusters of California poppies. The trail narrows again as you reach the largest poppy fields. The native California poppy is the official state flower, and California earned its reputation as the Golden State not only from the Gold Rush but also from these poppies, which turn the hills golden when they bloom. The flowers close at night and on overcast days, so the best time to see them is in the morning on a sunny day.

Continuing along the trail, you'll enjoy more blankets of wildflowers as you meander up and down and reach the end of the loop.

TURN-BY-TURN DIRECTIONS

1. From the trailhead, pass a wooden fence and take the clear trail marked for Weir Canyon. An interpretive display welcomes you to Santiago Oaks Regional Park.
2. At 0.1 miles, at a wide fork in the trail, head left on the Weir Canyon Trail.
3. At 0.3 miles, veer right on the Old Weir Canyon trail.
4. At a T-junction at 0.5 miles, go a few feet left and take a narrow, unmarked trail that continues uphill to the right.
5. Ignore all smaller offshoot trails until the main trail intersects an unmarked wide gravel path at 0.6 miles. Here, keep right, heading uphill.
6. Again, stay on the wide path and ignore all offshoot trails. At 1.1 miles, pass a large green water tank on the left.
7. At 1.9 miles, staying on the main trail, you'll see fields of poppies on either side (during the spring).
8. At 2.1 miles, take a sharp switchback to the left, following the main trail and ignoring a small side trail that continues straight.
9. At 2.3 miles, follow the Weir Canyon Trail to the left.
10. At 2.8 miles, continue straight ahead, ignoring a trail heading uphill on the right.
11. At 3.6 miles, ignore a trail on the left and continue straight to the larger intersection around 60 feet ahead that closes the loop. Here, veer left on the Weir Canyon Trail to head back down to the trailhead.

FIND THE TRAILHEAD

From downtown Anaheim, take CA-91 E. for around 10 miles to Exit 39 for Weir Canyon Rd. From the exit, turn right onto S. Weir Canyon Rd and continue for 0.7 miles. At S. Serrano Ave., turn right and continue for 2.0 miles. At Hidden Canyon Rd., turn left. After 0.5 miles, the road turns right and becomes E. Overlook Terrace. The trailhead is at this right turn. There is street parking on both sides of Hidden Canyon Rd. before you reach the trailhead and on both sides of E. Overlook Terrace once you pass the trailhead.

GREEN CHEEK BEER COMPANY

Co-owners and friends Brian Rauso and Evan Price opened Green Cheek Beer Company in June 2017. Price, the head brewer and creative side of the operation, began as a homebrewer in 2006 and worked at four different breweries before connecting with Rauso and opening Green Cheek. Price won prizes for his beers at his previous breweries, and Green Cheek has in turn won numerous notable awards and received national recognition.

Price continually tinkers with the beer recipes, so while the brewery always has varieties of light beer, IPA, and darker beer, the specific brews rotate to keep things interesting. One favorite that regularly makes the rounds is the Radiant Beauty West Coast IPA, which was the brewery's first beer to win silver medals at both the World Beer Cup and the Great American Beer Festival. The most recent iteration of Radiant Beauty is a double dry-hopped variation which layers Citra, Mosaic, and Simcoe hops to create a crisp and complex brew.

LAND MANAGER

Santiago Oaks Regional Park
2145 N. Windes Dr.
Orange, CA 92869
(714) 973-6620
www.ocparks.com/santiagooaks
Map: www.ocparks.com/sites/ocparks/files/2022-06/Santiago%20
Oaks%20Park%20Map%2022.06.10.pdf

BREWERY/RESTAURANT

Green Cheek Brewing Company
2294 N. Batavia St., Unit C
Orange, CA 92865
(714) 998-8172
www.greencheekbeer.com/#home

Distance from trailhead: 8.2 miles

BLACK STAR CANYON FALLS

AN ADVENTUROUS EXCURSION TO A STUNNING WATERFALL

SILVERADO

▷⋯ STARTING POINT	⋯✕ DESTINATION
BLACK STAR CANYON FALLS TRAILHEAD	**BLACK STAR CANYON FALLS**
🍺 BREWERY	🏁 HIKE TYPE
DIVINE SCIENCE BREWING	**STRENUOUS**
🐾 DOG FRIENDLY	📅 SEASON
YES (LEASH REQUIRED)	**NOVEMBER—MAY**
$ FEES	⏱ DURATION
NONE	**4 HOURS 45 MIN.**
⛰ MAP REFERENCE	↦ LENGTH
IRVINE RANCH OPEN SPACE	**7.6 MILES** (ROUND TRIP)
🔍 HIGHLIGHTS	〰 ELEVATION GAIN
WATERFALL	**879 FT**

PARTICLE HAZE HAZY IPA

HAZY STRAW

CITRUS, FRUITY

HOPPY, CITRUS

BITTERNESS

SWEETNESS

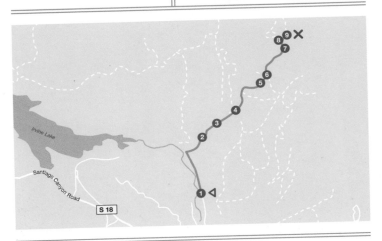

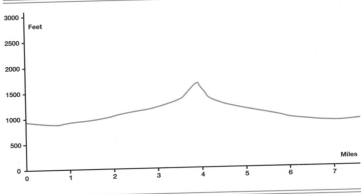

HIKE DESCRIPTION

Get your feet—and legs—wet on this adventurous excursion to a breathtaking 65-foot segmented waterfall. After the hike, revel in the experience over a gluten-free IPA at Divine Science Brewing.

This hike is for adventure seekers who aren't afraid to get dirty. The out-and-back trail requires plenty of problem-solving and delicate foot—and hand—placements starting around two and a half miles in, but the extra effort adds to the experience. The trail begins on a wide dirt road in Black Star Canyon Wilderness Park, which is managed by the city of Irvine, but around two miles in, the road transitions into the Cleveland National Forest. You'll follow the main wide dirt road meandering through chaparral shrubland with occasional shade from oak and eucalyptus trees.

When you turn off the main dirt road, you'll head down a steep trail leading to a creek. Here the adventure really begins with a series of challenging creek crossings. Just how challenging these crossings are will depend on the water level: after heavy rains, much of the hike becomes creek walking in water that can get up to thigh-high. On hot days, the cold water feels very nice. Wear shoes and clothes that you're comfortable getting wet in, and enjoy the experience. Trekking poles can help you keep your balance and test the water depth.

As you cross and recross the creek, the trail leads you through a lush riparian corridor. Riparian zones are ecosystems near waterways; this one provides essential habitat for a diverse lineup of native species including laurel sumac, coastal live oak, and poison oak (careful!). As you get closer to the falls, you'll pass through two areas outfitted with ropes to help you climb up small boulder sections and keep your footing on slippery mud slopes. The first rope will be on the right side of the river; the second is on the left.

You'll reach Black Canyon Falls a few minutes after traversing the second roped section. While the waterfall typically dries up in the summer and fall, after a heavy rain or overall wet season it puts on a phenomenal show. The water falls from two sources: a central point approximately 65 feet above the base and a hole lower down on the left around fifteen feet above the ground. This hole was created in the 1870s as a mining shaft by the Black Star Coal Mining Company.

TURN-BY-TURN DIRECTIONS

1. From the parking area, follow the paved road to where it ends at a metal gate with a sign for Black Star Canyon. Start along the wide dirt road. Ignore several closed trails to the left and right and stay on the main road.

2. At 1.1 miles, pass a sign saying "Leaving OC Parks Property" and continue on the road. To the left and right, you'll see several closed private roads. Ignore these and stay on the primary road.

3. At 1.5 miles, cross a metal bridge over the river.

4. At 1.9 miles, cross another bridge with metal railings.

5. At 2.7 miles, leave the main road and follow a narrow downhill trail marked with a metal sign for Black Star Canyon Falls. The trail will lead down to the creek in around 50 feet. Here, you'll have your first creek crossing and likely get your feet wet.

6. From here, follow what looks most like a trail and at each creek crossing look for the trail on the other side. The trail will never stray too far from the creek, so when in doubt, stay close to the creek.

7. At 3.6 miles, on the right side of the creek, find a rope tied to a tree to assist with scrambling up some boulders.

8. At around 3.8 miles, on the left side of the creek, follow a rope up a steep slope among tree roots that can be muddy and slippery.

9. At 3.9 miles, follow the trail around the corner of a boulder and find the falls straight ahead. Return the way you came.

FIND THE TRAILHEAD

From Irvine, head northeast on Jamboree Rd. After around 2.5 miles, continue straight onto CA-261 (toll road). After 5.7 miles, take Exit 6A for Santiago Cyn Rd. and Chapman Ave. and then turn right onto Santiago Cyn Rd. After 5.4 miles, turn left onto Silverado Canyon Rd. and follow it for 0.1 miles. Turn left onto Black Star Canyon Rd. After 1.1 miles, reach trailhead parking on both sides of the road. The trailhead is at a gate that blocks cars from continuing along the road.

DIVINE SCIENCE BREWING

Co-owners Domonic and Robert Keifer, both of whom have gluten sensitivities, founded Divine Science Brewing to produce great gluten-free beer. They opened their taproom in February 2022, but have been selling their beer throughout California since 2018. Divine Science labels itself as a "gypsy brewery," which means it has no brewing facility of its own and travels and pays to brew its beer at another brewer's facility. This form of brewing gives Divine Science the flexibility to experiment with different equipment and expand when needed.

All of the brewery's beer names and label artwork pay tribute to strong women in history and especially to women brewers, who were seen as witches in the Middle Ages. The triple dry-hopped Hazy IPA Particle Haze pays homage to San Lau Wu, a female physicist who played a key role in discovering the Higgs boson and completing the Standard Model of particle physics.

LAND MANAGER

Irvine Ranch Open Space
13333 Black Star Canyon Rd.
Silverado, CA 92676
(714) 973-6696
www.ocparks.com/irvine-ranch-open-space
Map: www.ocparks.com/sites/ocparks/files/2021-05/Open_Space_map.pdf

BREWERY/RESTAURANT

Divine Science Brewing
15481 Red Hill Ave. Ste C
Tustin, CA 92780
(562) 640-1405
www.divinesciencebrewing.com/

Distance from trailhead: 15.5 miles

LAUREL CANYON

HIKE UP A CANYON TO A STUNNING OCEAN VIEW

LAGUNA BEACH

▷⋯ STARTING POINT	⋯✕ DESTINATION
WILLOW STAGING AREA	**BOMMER RIDGE**
🍺 BREWERY	🗺 HIKE TYPE
LAGUNA BEACH BEER COMPANY	**MODERATE**
🐾 DOG FRIENDLY	📅 SEASON
NO	**YEAR-ROUND**
$ FEES	🕐 DURATION
YES	**2 HOURS**
⛰ MAP REFERENCE	↦ LENGTH
POSTED AT TRAILHEAD	**5.1 MILES** (LOOP)
🔍 HIGHLIGHTS	∿ ELEVATION GAIN
OCEAN VIEWS, EMOJI ROCK	**791 FT**

TUAVA GUAVA HEFEWEIZEN

 HAZY PINK

 GUAVA, WHEAT

 GUAVA, SOUR

BITTERNESS SWEETNESS

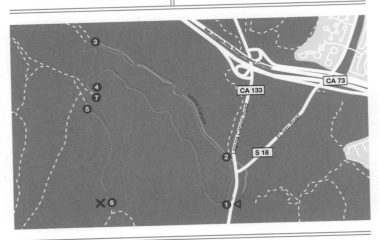

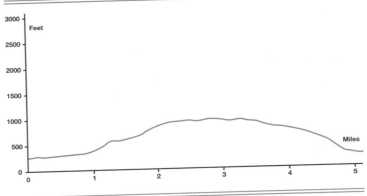

HIKE DESCRIPTION

Explore this pristine wilderness area featuring rocks and fossils that are millions of years old. At the ridge, take in sweeping views out to the ocean. Then head back down for a refreshing guava hefeweizen from Laguna Beach Beer Company.

Orange County Parks puts in a huge effort to maintain its extensive park system and it shows in Laguna Coast Wilderness Park—7,000 acres of wilderness with 40 miles of trails leading through coastal canyons and along ridgelines with breathtaking ocean vistas. The park is a part of the South Coast Wilderness, which includes other neighboring parks and comprises almost 20,000 acres of wild land. The multi-use trail system is well maintained, with clear trail markers, a free interpretive audio tour, and regular free guided hikes focusing on fitness, geology, families, or native species. If you'd like to learn more about the history of the land, geology, and native species, bring along headphones and a charged phone to dial into the twenty-four posted audio stops along this route.

As you set out from the parking lot, you'll immediately see sandstone boulders with interesting formations cropping out alongside the trail. The shapes of the rocks have evolved over millions of years of erosion in the rain and wind. Walking along the flat, rocky first section of trail, you'll see grasslands and shrubs that flourish in the spring with wildflowers like blue dicks, monkeyflower, and purple owl's clover.

Within the first half-mile, the trail gives way to oak woodlands that create a shaded tunnel. This is the Laurel Canyon hikers-only section, so you don't need to worry about bikers. As you emerge from the tunnel, notice a rock on the right that looks distinctly like a face sticking its tongue out. On Google Maps, the rock is aptly named Emoji Rock, though it's also commonly called Ghost Rock.

Continuing along the often-dry creek bed, the trail gains elevation until it comes out onto the wider multi-use Laurel Spur Trail. Here the climb begins up to the Bommer Ridge Trail. When you come out onto Bommer Ridge, if it's a clear day, you'll be rewarded with a gorgeous view of Emerald Canyon and the ocean. However, the trail is often foggy and presents a more mysterious experience. In fact, summer fog is so common in this area that residents call it "June Gloom" (and sometimes "Gray May" and "No Sky July"). Water evaporates from the ocean, creating the fog, and as the warm inland air rises, the fog is sucked into its place. This is a normal part of summer in California, and some native species like seaside lupine and coastal redwood have adapted to collect moisture from the fog.

From Bommer Ridge, you can continue left or right for several miles and connect to other trails all the way out to the ocean if you choose. Our route only goes a short distance along the ridge to appreciate the view, then turns around and completes the loop down the wide dirt Willow Canyon Road Trail.

TURN-BY-TURN DIRECTIONS

1. From the Willow Staging Area (parking lot), head up the main trail. 100 feet down the trail, take a right onto the Laurel Canyon Trail.
2. At 0.3 miles, keep left on the Laurel Canyon Trail.
3. At 1.5 miles, head left on the Laurel Spur Trail and continue to stay left, ignoring the Lizard Trail on the right around 150 feet up the path.
4. At a T-junction at 2.0 miles, turn right onto the Willow Canyon Road Trail and continue straight, ignoring the Bommer Spur Trail on the right.
5. At a T-junction at 2.2 miles, turn left onto the Bommer Ridge Trail. Follow the Bommer Ridge Trail up along the ridge and around a small curve.
6. At 2.8 miles, turn around and return to the Willow Canyon Road Trail turnoff; turn right on the Willow Canyon Road Trail.
7. At 3.6 miles, continue straight on the Willow Canyon Road Trail. Follow it back to the Willow Staging Area.

FIND THE TRAILHEAD

From Irvine, take I-405 S towards San Diego. After 3.3 miles, take the exit for CA-133 and keep right for CA-133 S towards Laguna Beach. Merge onto CA-133 S and proceed for 4.9 miles. After passing through the stoplight intersection with El Toro Rd., you'll see the Willow Canyon trailhead parking on the right.

The parking lot has somewhat restrictive hours and the park closes in rainy or muddy conditions, so be sure to check the OC Parks website before setting out.

From Laguna Beach, you can take the 89 bus up Laguna Canyon Rd., which will drop you off across the street from the parking lot. This bus also stops in front of Laguna Beach Beer Company.

LAGUNA BEACH BEER COMPANY

Co-owners Christian Emsiek, Brent Reynard, and Mikey Lombardo started Laguna Beach Beer Co. as a local community space dedicated to the appreciation of craft beer. The team opened their first location and primary brewing facility in Rancho Santa Margarita in 2017 and opened the Laguna Canyon Road taproom in 2018. The taproom offers woodfired pizzas, deli-style sandwiches, and a variety of refreshing beers.

Emsiek manages all the operations and brewing. On his time off you can find him hiking and mountain biking on the local trails—including those in Laguna Coast Wilderness Park. The brewery sponsors the local high school mountain-bike team and hosts regular live music on the patio. The tart, tropical, and refreshing Tuava Guava Hefeweizen is named after Tortuava Beach, a hidden spot in Laguna that you can only reach at low tide. Emsiek uses a bioengineered thiolized yeast strain from Berkeley Yeast to create this hazy, tropical, easy-drinking brew.

LAND MANAGER

Laguna Coast Wilderness Park
18751 Laguna Canyon Road
Laguna Beach, CA 92651
(949) 923-2235
www.ocparks.com/lagunacoast
Map: www.ocparks.com/sites/ocparks/files/2021-04/Laguna%20
Coast%20Wilderness%20Park%20Map.pdf

BREWERY/RESTAURANT

Laguna Beach Beer Company
859 Laguna Canyon Road
Laguna Beach, CA 92651
(949) 715-0805
lagunabeach.lagunabeer.com/

Distance from trailhead: 2.7 miles

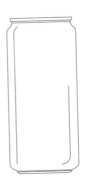

SAN DIEGO

PARADISE MOUNTAIN

A CHALLENGING WORKOUT
WITH PANORAMIC MOUNTAIN VIEWS

VALLEY CENTER

▷··· STARTING POINT	···✕ DESTINATION
HELLHOLE CANYON PRESERVE PARKING	**PARADISE MOUNTAIN**
🍺 BREWERY	🗺 HIKE TYPE
RINCON RESERVATION ROAD BREWERY	**STRENUOUS**
🐾 DOG FRIENDLY	📅 SEASON
YES (LEASH REQUIRED)	**SEPTEMBER—JULY**
$ FEES	⏱ DURATION
NONE	**4 HOURS**
⛰ MAP REFERENCE	↦ LENGTH
HELLHOLE CANYON PRESERVE BROCHURE	**8.7 MILES** (LOLLIPOP LOOP)
🔍 HIGHLIGHTS	〰 ELEVATION GAIN
MOUNTAIN VIEWS, NATIVE AMERICAN—OWNED BREWERY	**1,936 FEET**

TROPICAL OASIS
BLONDE ALE

4.2 %
ALCOHOL
CONTENT

 STRAW

 TROPICAL,
FRUITY

 PEACH,
GUAVA

BITTERNESS   SWEETNESS

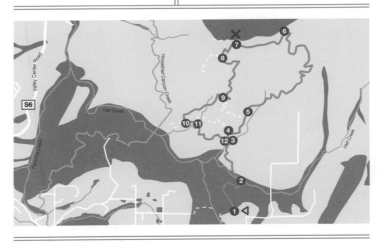

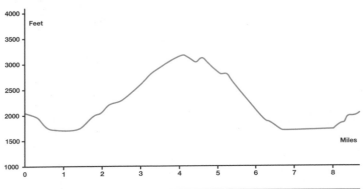

HIKE DESCRIPTION

 Discover a challenging hike with pristine views nestled among Native American reservations. After working up a sweat, enjoy a refreshing tropical brew at the United States' first and only certified Native American owned and operated brewery on tribal land.

The Hellhole Canyon Preserve gets its name from the area's extreme heat during the summer. It's closed in August due to the high temperatures, but at other times of the year provides a welcoming getaway from more crowded parks in San Diego County. Wildfires in 2003 and 2007 have dramatically affected the preserve's landscape. In 2003, a wildfire destroyed the entire area and forced the preserve to close for a full year. In the fires' wake, native plants have been growing back through the natural succession process, providing a unique view into a specially adapted ecosystem.

The hike begins on a wide path and drops around 300 feet of elevation in the first mile. Along the path you'll see small signs introducing various native plant species such as Mission Manzanita and Laurel Sumac. At various points throughout the hike, you'll also find larger interpretive displays about the area's natural history, with details about bobcats, mountain lions, wildfire, birds of prey, and a three-dimensional topographic map of Hellhole Canyon.

Around three-quarters of a mile into the hike, you'll cross Hell Creek, which flows most of the year and supports the oak woodland and riparian habitats. As you move out of the oak trees and begin the uphill climb to Paradise Mountain, the landscape transforms to dense chaparral. During wet years, in late winter and spring, the hillsides and shrubs lining the trail come alive with clumps of white and blue California lilac flowers. Specifically adapted to the wildfire-prone ecosystem, California lilac seeds have extremely hard outer shells that actually require fire for germination. To help the fire-induced germination, lilac leaves are coated with flammable resins that encourage fire. While the above-ground part of the plant may burn, it can regrow quickly from the roots.

After the first mile you'll embark on a three-and-a-half-mile uphill push to the summit of Paradise Mountain. The summit itself is not marked and is rather nondescript, but all along the ridge from the end of the third mile onward, you'll get panoramic views of the surrounding mountains. Looking northwest, you'll see a few large buildings below: Harrah's Resort and the Rincon Reservation Road Brewery.

After the summit, the trail makes a steep descent. You'll pass two optional viewpoints, near the summit and about half a mile past it. As you get to the end of the descent, you'll cross a dry creek bed lined with California lilacs. After a more gradual descent through chaparral, you'll cross a small ravine. The loop closes as you traverse a windy section with a mild dropoff on the right. From here, you'll make the final push uphill through laurel sumac and more California lilacs to the parking lot.

TURN-BY-TURN DIRECTIONS

1. From the parking lot, pass the bathrooms and follow the only path leading into the brush.
2. At 0.7 miles, cross Hell Creek.
3. At 1.3 miles, reach the start of the loop, where you'll find a posted map and trail sign. Go right on the Horsethief Trail.
4. At 1.4 miles, veer right on the Paradise Mountain Trail.
5. At a T-junction at 1.8 miles, take a sharp right, staying on the Paradise Mountain Trail. On the small map posted at the junction, this will be the orange dotted line.
6. At 3.9 miles, follow the arrow for the trail on the left.
7. At 4.6 miles, reach the summit. This is not clearly marked, but you'll have views on all sides. Around 200 feet further on, reach a fork with a sign for Viewpoint One on the right. Stay left here (after checking out the viewpoint if you wish!)
8. At 5.0 miles, leave Viewpoint Two on the right and continue left on the Rodriguez Trail. (Again, feel free to check out the viewpoint if you wish!)
9. At 6.0 miles, keep right on the Rodriguez Trail.
10. At 6.7 miles, continue straight ahead in the direction of Hell Creek Trail Staging (the parking lot), ignoring a trail on the right.
11. At 6.8 miles, continue straight following the arrows for Hell Creek Trail Staging (simply labeled "Staging" on the sign) and ignoring a trail on the left.
12. At 7.4 miles, reach the start of the loop and turn right to return to the parking lot.

FIND THE TRAILHEAD

From Escondido, head northeast on W Grand Ave. After 2.7 miles, turn left onto Bear Valley Pkwy. and continue for 0.7 miles. When the road meets Valley Pkwy., turn right. After 1.3 miles, turn right onto Lake Wohlford Rd. and continue for 5.9 miles. Turn right onto Paradise Mountain Rd. and continue for 3.3 miles. At a six-way intersection, take the second left onto Kiavo Dr. and continue for 0.5 miles. When this road ends at a T-junction, turn left onto Santee Ln., entering Hellhole Canyon preserve. This road ends at the parking lot.

RINCON RESERVATION ROAD BREWERY

Rincon Reservation Road Brewery, often called 3R, is the first Native American brewery on tribal land in the U.S. It is owned and operated by the Rincon Band of Luiseño Indians, who are known as the original Californians and have lived in the area for over 14,000 years. The Rincon Band of Luiseño Indians opened the brewery in 2016 as SR76 next to Rincon-owned Harrah's Resort and Casino as another way to expand the tribe's reach. In 2019 the brewery rebranded to Rincon Reservation Road Brewery, honoring a trail the Luiseño people used to travel along from the area of Palomar Mountain to modern-day Oceanside, hunting, gathering food, and visiting other villages along the route. The brewery itself has fourteen taps and hosts regular events like karaoke, live music, and trivia. Its Tropical Oasis has quickly become a favorite easy drinker. The Tropical Oasis uses the original Oasis blonde ale base with fruity additions including peach, passionfruit, strawberry, and orange.

LAND MANAGER

Hellhole Canyon County Preserve
19324 Santee Lane
Valley Center, CA 92082
(760) 742-1631
www.sdparks.org/content/sdparks/en/park-pages/HellholeCanyon.html
Map: www.sdparks.org/content/dam/sdparks/en/pdf/Brochures
Miscellaneous/2018_Hellhole_Canyon_Brochure_FINAL.pdf

BREWERY/RESTAURANT

Rincon Reservation Road Brewery
777 Harrah's Rincon Way
Valley Center, CA 92082
(760) 651-6572
www.3rbrewery.com

Distance from trailhead: 9.3 miles

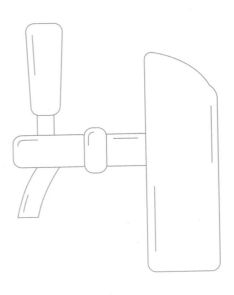

POTATO CHIP ROCK

DISCOVER ONE OF THE MOST ICONIC SOUTHERN CALIFORNIA HIKES TO A THIN ROCK OUTCROP

POWAY

▷··· STARTING POINT	···✕ DESTINATION
LAKE POWAY RD.	**MOUNT WOODSON**
🍺 BREWERY	🗺 HIKE TYPE
SECOND CHANCE BEER COMPANY	**MODERATE/ STRENUOUS**
🐾 DOG FRIENDLY	📅 SEASON
YES (LEASH REQUIRED)	**YEAR-ROUND**
$ FEES	🕐 DURATION
YES (ON WEEKENDS)	**4 HOURS**
⛰ MAP REFERENCE	↦ LENGTH
POSTED AT TRAILHEAD	**7.7 MILES** (ROUND TRIP)
👁 HIGHLIGHTS	〰 ELEVATION GAIN
SUMMIT VIEWS, OCEAN VIEWS	**2,169 FEET**

FLUFFY TANGER-INE CLOUDS HAZY IPA

7.0 % ALCOHOL CONTENT

 HAZY STRAW

 TANGERINE, CITRUS

 TANGERINE, CREAMY

BITTERNESS

SWEETNESS

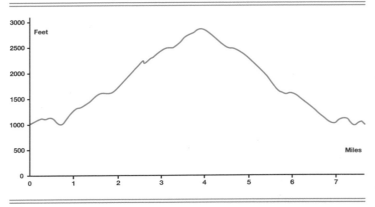

HIKE DESCRIPTION

This challenging hike leads to one of the most popular outdoorsy photo opportunities in Southern California. After working hard on the hike, choose from among a wide variety of unique beers at the dog-loving Second Chance Beer Company.

Potato Chip Rock is a unique formation of thin granodiorite—a type of igneous rock—that sticks out from a huge boulder over the void like a giant potato chip. This formation was likely created when a large part of the boulder broke off and fell down the slope, leaving the potato chip sliver hovering eighty feet above the ground. The attraction has become so popular that in the spring and summer on weekends there is regularly a line of over fifty people waiting to take a picture on the rock. For less of a line and no parking fee, go mid-week.

After a tough three and a half miles hiking up the steep, rocky, and sandy Mount Woodson Trail, you'll see the potato chip sticking out ahead like a magic carpet or flying saucer. After one more switchback, you'll reach the chip in earnest. To get the iconic photo on the rock, you'll have to do some scrambling and rock jumping. While people regularly take pictures posing and doing different stunts on this outcrop, keep in mind that it's a natural rock structure and could break at any point—so stand on it at your own risk.

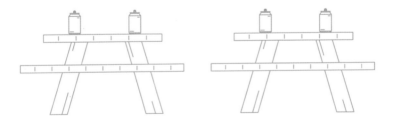

Aside from Potato Chip Rock, this hike offers a fun and rewarding challenge winding along switchbacks and climbing rocky stairs. Be sure to regularly stop and look behind you on the way up to enjoy the expansive views of Lake Poway, the surrounding hills, and the Pacific Ocean. The trail mostly leads through chaparral and is hardly shaded at all, making it very hot during the summer. In late winter and spring, you'll find head-height native hoaryleaf ceanothus bushes speckled with white flowers lining parts of the trail.

If you stick around till towards evening and then head down, you'll be able to see the sun sinking towards (and then into) the ocean in the distance almost the whole way down.

TURN-BY-TURN DIRECTIONS

1. From the parking lot just before the bathrooms, take the Lake Poway Trail.
2. At 0.1 miles, veer right following the marked post to a scenic overlook. After around 400 feet, ignore an unmarked trail on the right and continue straight, overlooking the lake.
3. At 0.3 miles, pass through an intersection with port-a-potties and continue straight ahead.
4. At 0.5 miles, pass the Sumac Trail heading uphill to the right. Do not follow it; continue going straight ahead.
5. At the fork at 0.7 miles, bear right on the Mt. Woodson Trail.
6. At 1.1 miles, stay left on the Mt. Woodson Trail.
7. At 1.5 miles, veer right to remain on the Mt. Woodson Trail.
8. At 1.8 miles, veer left on the Mt. Woodson Trail.
9. At 2.5 miles reach a sign marked "Ridge Junction." Follow the sign to the left for a lookout about 300 feet down the trail. From the lookout, return to Ridge Junction and then bear right on the Mt. Woodson Trail.
10. At 2.8 miles, stay right on the Mt. Woodson Trail.
11. At 3.3 miles, pass a sign saying, "END OF CITY MAINTAINED TRAIL."
12. At 3.6 miles, reach an unmarked fork and bear left, looking directly at Potato Chip Rock.
13. At 3.7 miles, reach Potato Chip Rock. Then continue as the trail turns into a paved road and winds around satellite towers.
14. At 3.9 miles, take a sharp right turn to reach the summit 100 feet up the fire road. Return the way you came, skipping the lookout extension at Ridge Junction.
15. At the port-a-potties at 7.3 miles, take the unmarked right instead of the original left to loop closer to the lake.
16. At 7.5 miles, keep left, heading away from the lake and back towards the parking lot.

FIND THE TRAILHEAD

From Escondido, take I-15 S to Exit 24 for Rancho Bernardo Rd. Turn left onto Rancho Bernardo Rd. and continue for 1.7 miles, at which point the road turns into Espola Rd. Continue on Espola Rd. for 2.3 miles; then turn left onto Lake Poway Rd. After around 0.5 miles, pass through the parking pay booth for Lake Poway Recreation Area. Continue for another 0.3 miles, passing three different parking areas, and park when you reach a sign that says "NO RV OR BUSES BEYOND THIS POINT" with a bathroom building on the right. On weekends, you may have to park in one of the earlier parking areas.

SECOND CHANCE BEER COMPANY

Second Chance Beer Company began as a second chance for co-founders Marty Mendiola and Virginia Morrison after leaving the Rock Bottom Brewery in La Jolla (now closed). However, the name doubles as a nod to their ethos around giving back, specifically to dog-rescue organizations in California and Arizona. Since its founding in 2015, the small brewery has donated over $322,000 to dog-rescue and community organizations.

Fluffy Tangerine Clouds is one of the brewery's core brews. It has a hazy IPA base to which the brewers add oat malt, tangerine puree, and organic agave to get a full-bodied, sweet beer with clear notes of tangerine.

LAND MANAGER

Lake Poway Recreation Area
14644 Lake Poway Road
Poway, CA 92064
(858) 668-4772
www.poway.org/401/Lake-Poway
Map: www.poway.org/DocumentCenter/View/8013/Poway-Trails-Guide-and-Map-2020

BREWERY/RESTAURANT

Second Chance Beer Company
15378 Avenue of Science #222
San Diego, CA 92128
(858) 705-6250
www.secondchancebeer.com/

Distance from trailhead: 7.1 miles

ANNIE'S CANYON

EXPLORE A SLOT CANYON AND INTERTIDAL ZONE

SOLANA BEACH

▷⋯ STARTING POINT	⋯✗ DESTINATION
SOLANA HILLS TRAILHEAD	**ANNIE'S SLOT CANYON LOOKOUT**
🍺 BREWERY	🈺 HIKE TYPE
VIEWPOINT BREWING COMPANY	**MODERATE**
🐾 DOG FRIENDLY	📅 SEASON
YES (LEASH REQUIRED)	**YEAR-ROUND**
💲 FEES	🕐 DURATION
NONE	**1 HOUR 20 MIN.**
⛰ MAP REFERENCE	↦ LENGTH
POSTED AT TRAILHEAD	**2.5 MILES** (LOLLIPOP LOOP)
🔎 HIGHLIGHTS	〰 ELEVATION GAIN
SLOT CANYON, BIRD WATCHING	**466 FEET**

PENITENT MAN IPA

CLEAR GOLD

PINE, FRUITY

PINE, HOPPY

BITTERNESS

SWEETNESS

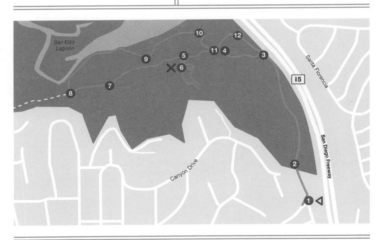

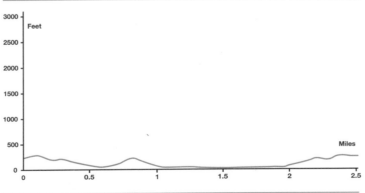

HIKE DESCRIPTION

Satisfy your thirst for adventure exploring this unique pocket of different environments, moving from a hidden slot canyon to an intertidal lagoon. Posthike, satisfy your physical thirst with a crisp West Coast IPA from the patio of Viewpoint Brewing Company.

Slot canyons like Annie's Canyon form during flooding over sandstone or sedimentary rock when water seeps into cracks in the rock. The water rushing through slowly erodes the rock and over millions of years, that erosion causes a deep channel along the crackline. The result is a naturally occurring maze weaving through the rock that towers above. The walls on either side showcase the many different layers of swirling rock that built up over millions of years when the rock formed. Some parts of the slot are no more than three feet wide, creating an isolated, otherworldly feeling. These slot canyons are notably rare around the world, but are uniquely common in the southwestern U.S. because of the sandstone and frequent flooding.

This hike has seen exponential growth in popularity since it officially opened in 2016. Due to its easy accessibility, the trail can often become overcrowded and the narrow slots can lead to backups that create long lines. To avoid the longest lines, go during off-peak times like early mornings, weekdays, or winter. It's even better if you can manage all three.

As you set off down the wide gravel road from a residential side street adjacent to the massive, eleven-lane I-5, it's hard to imagine anything spectacular ahead. After descending around 200 feet next to a shoulder-height chain-link fence and chaparral shrubland, you'll head onto a smaller trail lined with golden wattle. The golden wattle is a tall shrub or short tree native to southeastern Australia and is the national flower of Australia. Decades ago, people in the area planted golden wattle in the San Elijo Ecological Reserve to shelter and obscure a hunting lodge that was once there. Now, the golden wattles bloom with thousands of bright yellow puffball-like flowers in late winter.

Around three-quarters of a mile in, you'll reach the start of the slot canyon, where you'll find the first sandstone wall covered with carved initials and phrases. These markings are, sadly, from people taking advantage of the soft rock over the years, but the area used to be much worse—before it officially opened in 2016, it was covered in spray-painted graffiti and trash. Thanks to a local resident named Annie—the canyon's namesake—who led the restoration efforts to clean up the canyon, the walls are now clean and offer a more natural experience. Anyone with claustrophobia should be aware that this part of the trail gets into tight spaces with sandstone walls on either side. In some spots you'll find metal ladders or steps you'll need to climb. When you come out of the slot canyon, you'll emerge above the rock and be rewarded with a view of the San Elijo lagoon and out to the Pacific Ocean.

After going through the slot canyon and descending via a series of switchbacks, you'll walk along the lagoon, one of San Diego's largest wetlands. The salt marsh swells with the tides twice a day and then reduces to mudflats. The mudflats are a nutrient-rich landscape for a diverse range of birds, and you may see a number of endangered or threatened species such as light-footed clapper rails, California least terns, and snowy plovers.

TURN-BY-TURN DIRECTIONS

1. From the end of Solana Hills Drive, pass through a chain-link gate and find a bulletin board with a trail map and information.
2. At 0.1 miles, ignore a small trail spur on the left and continue straight, following the main unmarked trail.
3. At 0.4 miles, veer left onto the Annie's Canyon Trail.
4. At 0.6 miles, keep left at an unmarked T-junction. 200 feet further on, reach a fork in the trail and keep left again, still following the Annie's Canyon Trail.

5. At 0.7 miles, reach a large junction and interpretive display. Continue left on the Annie's Canyon Trail, passing through a metal fence. At a T-junction 200 feet later, go right on the signposted Slot Canyon to Viewpoint Trail. This is where the slot canyon starts.

6. Follow the loop until it brings you back to the start of the slot canyon at 1.0 miles. Here, turn right, returning to the large junction in Step 5. Now turn left on the unmarked trail heading west. Continue straight ahead, ignoring two smaller trails on the right.

7. At the fork at 1.2 miles, veer right.

8. At a T-junction at 1.3 miles, veer right on the unmarked trail leading back up along the San Elijo Lagoon.

9. At 1.6 miles, keep left on the unmarked trail to continue along the lagoon.

10. At 1.8 miles, keep right on the unmarked trail to loop back up to the Annie's Canyon Trail.

11. At 1.9 miles, reach the T-junction you passed at 0.6 miles. Turn left and then, at the next junction in 200 feet, veer left, leaving your original trail.

12. At 2.0 miles, connect with the wider unmarked trail going right. Stay on this trail until you return to the trailhead.

FIND THE TRAILHEAD

From San Diego, get on I-5 N and continue for around 20 miles until you reach Exit 37 for Lomas Santa Fe Dr. Turn left onto Lomas Santa Fe Dr. After 0.2 miles, turn right onto Solana Hills Dr. The trailhead will be at the end of this road in 0.3 miles. Park along this street or on one of the side streets to the left before the dead end.

VIEWPOINT BREWING COMPANY

Viewpoint Brewing Co is known for its back patio with a superb view of San Dieguito Lagoon and its wide variety of craft brews. Founded by Charles Koll with head brewer Moe Katomski in 2017 on the site of a local pottery studio (note the hanging planters, all made by the retired potter), the brewery has a full-service menu with favorites including the backyard burger and award-winning mac and cheese. With twenty to twenty-four rotating beers along with hard cider and hard kombucha options, the brewery has something for every preference. Koll and Katomski's goal for their beers from the beginning was drinkability, bridging the gap between macro drinkers and craft drinkers, but as they've developed, so have their beers, which range from the classic light, crushable lager styles to more complex IPAs, stouts, and darker beers.

The Penitent Man West Coast IPA is Viewpoint's number-one selling beer. Named after artist Dead Bronco's song Penitent Man, this beer is dry and hoppy with an impressively piney taste and a clean, crisp finish.

LAND MANAGER

San Elijo Lagoon Ecological Reserve
2710 Manchester Avenue
Cardiff-by-the-Sea, CA 92007
(760) 634-3026
www.sdparks.org/content/sdparks/en/park-pages/SanElijo.html
Map: www.sdparks.org/content/dam/sdparks/en/pdf/Brochures
Miscellaneous/SanElijoBrochure.pdf

BREWERY/RESTAURANT

Viewpoint Brewing Company
2201 San Dieguito Dr Suite D
Del Mar, CA 92014
(858)-356-9346
www.viewpointbrewing.com/

Distance from trailhead: 2.6 miles

COWLES MOUNTAIN

A STEEP HIKE TO VIEWS OVERLOOKING SAN DIEGO

SAN DIEGO

▷··· STARTING POINT	···✗ DESTINATION
BARKER WAY TRAILHEAD	COWLES MOUNTAIN
🍺 BREWERY	HIKE TYPE
PIZZA PORT OCEAN BEACH	**MODERATE**
🐾 DOG FRIENDLY	📅 SEASON
YES (LEASH REQUIRED)	YEAR-ROUND
$ FEES	🕐 DURATION
NONE	**1 HOUR 45 MIN.**
⛰ MAP REFERENCE	↦ LENGTH
POSTED AT TRAILHEAD	**3.1 MILES** (LOOP)
👁 HIGHLIGHTS	〜 ELEVATION GAIN
OCEAN VIEWS, SAN DIEGO VIEWPOINT	**866 FEET**

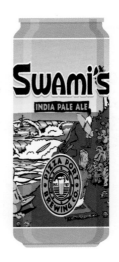

SWAMI'S IPA

STRAW

BISCUIT, HOPPY

DRY, CITRUS

BITTERNESS

SWEETNESS

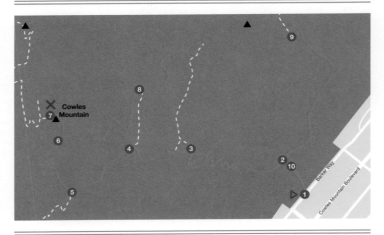

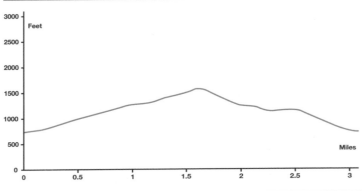

HIKE DESCRIPTION

Hike to the highest point in the city of San Diego for views overlooking the city and out to the ocean. Afterward, head to Ocean Beach for pizza and an iconic brew from Pizza Port.

Cowles Mountain (properly pronounced KOHLZ, but commonly pronounced KOWLZ) is one of the most popular hikes in San Diego. Mission Trails Regional Park keeps the trails well maintained. There are several trails of varying difficulty that head up the 1,591-foot peak, so you can choose the option that best suits you.

The Barker Way Trail is a happy medium with regard to crowds and difficulty. The trailhead is off a side street and has a port-a-potty and information board. You'll soon reach about half a mile of steep switchbacks weaving up the hillside. The native shrub woollyleaf ceanothus lines parts of the trail for the first mile and has beautiful clusters of blue flowers blooming in the winter, or occasionally in the spring, if the rain comes late. During wetter years, the blooms can be particularly abundant and can turn entire areas blue.

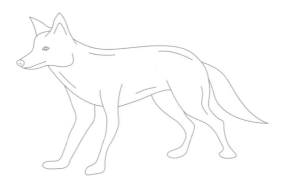

After about a mile, the Barker Way Trail converges with the Cowles Mountain Trail. Here you'll find another set of challenging switchbacks, with wooden fencing to prevent hikers from taking shortcuts and eroding the trail. As you climb, you'll enjoy views looking over the city and Lake Murray, and, on a clear day, out to the ocean.

After you reach the top, you'll loop around the other side of Cowles Mountain along the wide gravel Cowles Service Trail, which will return you to the Barker Way trailhead. (If you want to extend the hike from the top of Cowles Mountain, continue to Pyles Peak before turning around.) Throughout the hike, look out for animals like rattlesnakes, desert cottontail rabbits, coyotes, and even bobcats.

This is a great night hike when there's a full moon, as you'll see the moon rise dramatically over the hills to the east. (Just remember to bring a headlamp!)

TURN-BY-TURN DIRECTIONS

1.   From the trailhead off Barker Way, follow the sign for the Cowles Service Road Trail and the Barker Way Trail.
2.   At the fork at 0.1 miles, bear left, following the Barker Way Trail.
3.   At 0.7 miles, reach a fork in the road and continue to the left, following signs for Cowles Mountain summit.
4.   At 0.9 miles, stay left, following the Barker Way Trail.
5.   At 1.1 miles, reach the intersection with the Cowles Mountain Trail and turn right onto the Cowles Mountain Trail headed towards the summit.
6.   At 1.5 miles, stay left and continue on the switchbacks, ignoring an unmarked trail on the right.
7.   At 1.6 miles, reach the summit of Cowles Mountain. After enjoying the view, turn around and head right onto the Cowles Service Road Trail.
8.   At 2.1 miles, continue on the main wide road, ignoring a trail spur on the right.
9.   At 2.5 miles, pass a sign saying, "CAUTION YIELD TO FAST MOVING EMERGENCY VEHICLES." Ignore the Big Rock Trail on the left.
10. At 3.0 miles, arrive at the first intersection on the hike. Bear right and continue for 0.1 miles to return to the parking lot.

FIND THE TRAILHEAD

From Downtown San Diego, take CA-94 E for 7.7 miles. Stay left to take the CA-94 E and CA-125 N exit towards Spring St.; then keep left for Exit 9B for CA-125 N/Santee. Stay on CA-125 N for 3.7 miles until Exit 20A for Navajo Rd. Turn left on Navajo Rd. and continue for 0.8 miles. At Boulder Lake Ave., turn right and continue for 0.5 miles until the T-junction with Barker Way. Turn right on Barker Way. The trailhead will be on the left about 300 feet down the road.

PIZZA PORT OCEAN BEACH

Pizza Port was founded in 1987, when brother-and-sister team Vince and Gina Marsaglia bought a pizza place in Solana Beach. Vince began homebrewing in the restaurant's storage space, and they started offering craft beers in 1992. Since then, Pizza Port has won over ninety-one medals or awards at the Great American Beer Festival and has expanded to include six different brewpub locations, including this one in Ocean Beach. The Ocean Beach location has a fifteen-barrel serving tank that allows the beer to go directly from tank to tap. Head brewer Matt Palmer grew up in San Diego and takes pride in the laid-back, family-friendly environment of Ocean Beach's Pizza Port.

The Swami's IPA is one of the original beers that Pizza Port began selling in 1992. This West Coast–style IPA is named after a local surf break just below a self-realization fellowship ashram around Encinitas.

LAND MANAGER

Mission Trails Regional Park
One Father Junipero Serra Trail
San Diego, CA 92119
(619) 668-3281
www.mtrp.org
Map: www.mtrp.org/wp-content/uploads/2022/10/MTRP_Trail_
Map_2022-10.pdf

BREWERY/RESTAURANT

Pizza Port Ocean Beach
1956 Bacon Street
Ocean Beach, CA 92107
(619) 224-4700
www.pizzaport.com/brewpubs/ocean-beach

Distance from trailhead: 15.9 miles

CHICANO PARK URBAN ART WALK

A WALK AMONG THE BEAUTIFUL MURALS OF BARRIO LOGAN

BARRIO LOGAN

▷⋯ STARTING POINT	⋯✕ DESTINATION
MUJERES BREW HOUSE	**CHICANO PARK**
🍺 BREWERY	🔁 HIKE TYPE
MUJERES BREW HOUSE	**EASY** 🚶
🐾 DOG FRIENDLY	📅 SEASON
YES (LEASH REQUIRED)	**YEAR-ROUND**
$ FEES	🕐 DURATION
NONE	**1 HOUR 20 MIN.**
⛰ MAP REFERENCE	↦ LENGTH
CHICANO PARK MURAL MAP	**3.0 MILES (LOOP)**
🔍 HIGHLIGHTS	〰 ELEVATION GAIN
HISTORIC MURALS, WOMEN-OWNED BREWERY, LATINA-OWNED BREWERY	**102 FEET**

BUENAS VIBRAS BLONDE ALE

5.3 %
ALCOHOL CONTENT

LIGHT GOLDEN

FLORAL

LIGHT, CREAMY

BITTERNESS

SWEETNESS

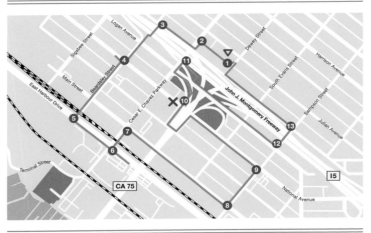

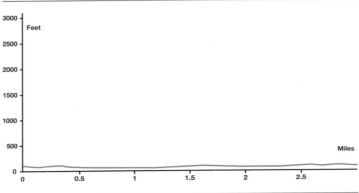

HIKE DESCRIPTION

Discover a window into Chicano culture during this easy urban hike through Barrio Logan. At the end of the walk, drop into the lively and welcoming women-centered Mujeres Brewery.

Barrio Logan has been designated one of fourteen California Cultural Districts for its authentic art, culture, and creativity. Over the past decade, this colorful area of San Diego has been growing in popularity and has become a hotspot for cute shops, delicious Chicano food, and a variety of craft breweries. On top of that, Chicano Park boasts the largest collection of Chicano murals in the world and is a National Historic Landmark. Many of the murals date back to 1973, three years after the community protested the construction of a highway patrol station in the already pre-allocated park area. The community occupied the space for twelve days and finally reached an agreement to acquire the site from the state for the development of a community park.

While I'm providing turn-by-turn directions for a specific route here, this is the most "make your own adventure" hike in this book. Don't be afraid to diverge from the designated route and explore the murals and the diverse neighborhood in whatever way you'd like. Follow what draws you in, take time to admire the paintings you find most powerful, and explore different side streets to discover murals that I haven't mentioned. If you want to learn more, you can join the Logan Barrio Art Crawl on the second Saturday of each month to explore local art galleries and enjoy live music and Chicano street food.

For more information on specific murals, duck into the Chicano Park Museum and Cultural Center.

This urban hike starts directly from Mujeres Brew House, but you can also access it about one mile in via the Barrio Logan light rail station.

TURN-BY-TURN DIRECTIONS

1. From the Mujeres Brew House, head south on Dewey St. towards the freeway, then turn right on the unmarked side street behind the brewery towards a long mural installation. Just past the first mural, you'll see Bread & Salt, an experimental art gallery with a 2021 mural by Tatiana Ortiz Rubio titled "Stop the Spread," depicting a woman with cempasúchil marigold flowers covering her nose and mouth.

2. At 0.1 miles, turn left on Cesar E Chavez Pkwy. At the stoplight the next block down before the highway underpass, turn right onto Kearny Ave.

3. At 0.3 miles, at the end of the block, take the pedestrian overpass on the right. Come out at the corner of Logan and Beardsley St. and continue straight on Beardsley St. On the first block on Beardsley St., you'll pass a corner mural on the right and a small painting on the left.

4. At 0.4 miles, at the intersection of Beardsley St. and National Ave., reach a small cloth mural installation around 150 feet down National Ave. on the right. Then return to Beardsley St. and continue down Beardsley St.

5. At 0.7 miles, cross the railroad tracks and E Harbor Dr. to reach a mural of shore birds; then turn left on E Harbor Dr.

6. At 0.9 miles, at the corner of E Harbor Dr. and Cesar E Chavez Pkwy., you'll find a large mural installation with two full-wall murals, the largest of which is on the Restaurant Depot building. Continue down E Harbor Dr. until the end of this long mural; then turn around and go right up Cesar E Chavez Pkwy.

7. At 1.1 miles, turn right onto Main St. On Main St., enjoy a collection of murals depicting Kokopelli, a Native American fertility deity who looks like a humpbacked flute player.

8. At 1.5 miles, turn left onto Sampson St.

9. At 1.6 miles, turn left on National Ave. This will lead you into Chicano Park, where you can enjoy a multitude of murals at your leisure, circling the different concrete freeway pillars. On the left, down Dewey St., there is a large fountain and skate park.

10. In the part of the park between National Ave. and Logan Ave., you'll find the Chicano Park Museum and Cultural Center, which provides historical background and explanations of many of the murals in the park.

11. At 2.2 miles, at the corner of Logan Ave. and Cesar E Chavez Pkwy., after loosely circling the park, turn right to see the murals along the walls of the underpass. Return to the Locan Ave. side of the underpass and turn back in the direction you came, walking next to the freeway along a small paved path decorated with a line of colorful murals. Continue down Logan Ave. back to Sampson St.

12. At 2.6 miles, turn left on Sampson St. and cross the freeway overpass.

13. At 2.7 miles, take a left on Kearny Ave. directly after crossing the freeway. Continue down Kearny Ave. to Dewey St., where you'll see Mujeres Brew House on the right.

FIND THE TRAILHEAD

To get to the start of this urban hike, you can drive directly to Mujeres Brew House and find parking either on Julian Ave. or Kearney Ave. From downtown San Diego, get on I-5 South and continue for 2.1 miles until the Cesar E Chavez Pkwy. exit. From the exit, turn left onto Logan Ave. At the next block, turn left onto Cesar E Chavez Pkwy. After 0.1 miles, turn right onto Julian Ave. At the next intersection, Mujeres Brew House will be on the right.

For a car-free option, you can take the light-rail blue train to the Barrio Logan stop. This will put you directly on the hike route. You'll start the hike at Step 6 in the turn-by-turn directions, stop at Mujeres Brew House along the way, and then complete the loop back to the train stop.

MUJERES BREW HOUSE

Mujeres Brew House started as a women's brew club to empower women of color interested in craft beer. Founder Carmen Velasco-Favela grew up in Barrio Logan and has become part of the positive growth throughout the neighborhood as trendy restaurants, coffee shops, and small businesses have created a lively, welcoming atmosphere. Velasco-Favela began the Mujeres Brew Club in collaboration with her husband's Border X Brewing, a Latino-owned brewery on the other side of the freeway that is also on this hike route and well worth a visit.

Today, the brewhouse is a colorful, welcoming space for women, by women (men are also welcome), and provides a venue for the community to gather for specialist markets and other community events like paint nights, loteria, and vision board planning. The brewery also features a number of beautiful women-centered murals created by local female artists. Head Brewer Samantha Olson likes to call her Buenas Vibras blonde ale a "blonde with highlights" because it has a residual sweetness due to a hazy strain of yeast.

LAND MANAGER

Chicano Park Steering Committee
P.O. Box 131050
San Diego, CA 92170
(619) 994-1345
www.chicanoparksandiego.com/index.html
Map: www.chicano-park.com/ChicanoParkMap.jpg

BREWERY/RESTAURANT

Mujeres Brew House
1983 Julian Avenue
San Diego, CA 92113
(619) 213-4340
www.mujeres-brew-house.business.site/?hl=en

Distance from trailhead: 0.0 miles

MOTHER MIGUEL MOUNTAIN

SEE NATIVE SPECIES AT THIS NATIONAL WILDLIFE REFUGE

CHULA VISTA

▷··· STARTING POINT

MOTHER MIGUEL MOUNTAIN TRAILHEAD

···✕ DESTINATION

MOTHER MIGUEL MOUNTAIN

🍺 BREWERY

CHULA VISTA BREWERY

🔀 HIKE TYPE

MODERATE

🐾 DOG FRIENDLY

YES (LEASH REQUIRED)

📅 SEASON

YEAR-ROUND

$ FEES

NONE

🕐 DURATION

2 HOURS 20 MIN.

⛰ MAP REFERENCE

POSTED AT TRAILHEAD

↦ LENGTH

4.4 MILES (ROUND TRIP)

👁 HIGHLIGHTS

OCEAN AND CITY VIEWS, VETERAN-, WOMAN-, AND BLACK- AND BROWN-OWNED BREWERY

〜 ELEVATION GAIN

1,040 FEET

CAN'T TOUCH THIS IMPERIAL RED ALE

AMBER

HOPS, CARMEL

MALTY, CARMEL

BITTERNESS   SWEETNESS

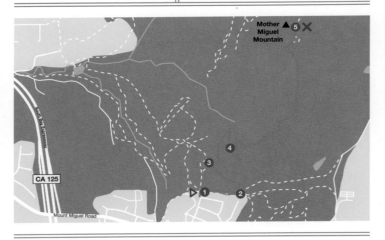

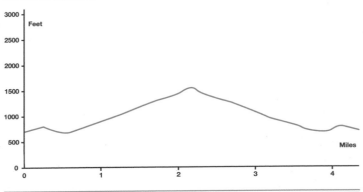

HIKE DESCRIPTION

Learn about this national wildlife refuge's native species while enjoying views that stretch from the nearby Sweetwater Reservoir to the Pacific Ocean and down to Mexico. Then quench your thirst at the local Chula Vista Brewery.

After rain, the San Diego National Wildlife Refuge becomes a lush, green oasis of rolling hills, wildflowers, and butterflies or caterpillars. In the summer, though, the Mother Miguel Mountain hike can be a relentlessly sunny and hot challenge with minimal shade coverage, so come prepared.

The first half-mile of the trail leads through San Diego Gas and Electric–owned land on a wide fire road. After a sharp right turn onto a smaller, singletrack dirt trail, you'll enter the official San Diego National Wildlife Refuge. Here, you'll find an interpretive display in both English and Spanish welcoming you to the refuge and the Mother Miguel Mountain Trail. A second interpretive display introduces one of the endangered species protected in the area: the Quino checkerspot butterfly, which has only been found in parts of Southern California and Mexico. There are two other interpretive displays further along the trail, one with updates on restoration and one dedicated to the surrounding views.

The trail then begins a series of small rocky switchbacks going up the mountain for about 0.7 miles. Due to the increase in its popularity, the trail has been severely eroded. With this in mind, please stay on the

trail as much as possible and don't take shortcuts. The trail will be undergoing sustainable redesign over the next few years to help reduce erosion.

The switchbacks straighten out after around a mile and a half, and then it's mostly straight uphill hiking among chaparral bushes to the summit. At the top you'll find an American flag and a POW/MIA flag that reads "YOU ARE NOT FORGOTTEN." From the summit you'll look down on the city of Chula Vista and out to the ocean in the west, northeast to the higher San Miguel Mountain (2559 ft), and south down to Mexico.

If you'd like to extend the hike, you can continue past the peak and follow one of the many trails leading down to the Sweetwater reservoir.

TURN-BY-TURN DIRECTIONS

1. From the trailhead directly off the road, follow the wide gravel trail for around 100 feet until you reach a junction with a metal gate. On the other side of the gate, take the wide fire road on the right.
2. At a fork at 0.2 miles, veer left on the unmarked service road. 30 feet down, stay left at another unmarked fork.
3. At 0.5 miles, take a small, unmarked trail on the right going off the main service road. This will lead to an interpretive display welcoming you to the Mother Miguel Mountain Trail. Here you'll cross a small wooden bridge over an often-dry creek bed.
4. Follow the switchbacks up the hill and the posted arrows for the next 1.5 miles.
5. At 2.2 miles, reach the American flag and POW/MIA flag at the peak. Return the way you came.

FIND THE TRAILHEAD

The trailhead begins at the end of Paseo Varacruz, though the best parking is in the lot for Mount San Miguel Park just off Paseo Varacruz around 0.1 miles before you reach the trailhead. To get here from downtown San Diego, head east on G St. for a mile and continue onto CA-94 E. Stay on CA-94 E for 7.7 miles until Exit 9A for CA-125 S (Toll Road). Continue on CA-125 S for 3.8 miles. At the fork with CA-54, keep right to stay on CA-125 S, following signs for Chula Vista. Continue for 2.9 miles and take Exit 9 for San Miguel Ranch Rd. Turn left on Mount Miguel Rd. After 0.7 miles, turn left onto Paseo Veracruz. After 0.1 miles, turn left onto Corte Ventura, entering Mount San Miguel Park. Park here and walk the 0.1 miles up Paseo Veracruz to the trailhead.

CHULA VISTA BREWERY

Chula Vista Brewery is one of the few Latina- and Black-owned breweries in Southern California. Husband-and-wife team and longtime Chula Vista residents Timothy and Dali Parker wanted to create a brewery for their community, and in May 2017 they opened the doors of their 3rd Avenue location. With the help of head brewer James Hodge, Chula Vista has won a number of awards, including the silver medal for Imperial Red Ale at the 2021 San Diego International Beer Competition with Can't Touch This. Can't Touch This is sweet, malty, and caramelly with a floral and fruity hop flavor.

Look out as well for the team's regularly changing collaboration brews like Lavender Honey Ale and barrel-aged stout. Many of the brewery's collaborations are with local Chula Vista businesses and nonprofit organizations supporting veterans—a nod to Timothy's background in the Navy.

LAND MANAGER

San Diego National Wildlife Refuge
14715 Highway 94
Jamul, CA 91935-3805
(619) 476-9150
www.fws.gov/refuge/san-diego/about-us
Map: www.fws.gov/media/mother-miguel-mountain-trail-map

BREWERY/RESTAURANT

Chula Vista Brewery
294 3rd Avenue,
Chula Vista, CA 91910
(619) 616-8806
www.chulavistabrewery.com/

Distance from trailhead: 8 miles

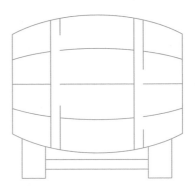

VIEJAS MOUNTAIN

A SHORT BUT CHALLENGING HIKE TO OUTSTANDING VIEWS

ALPINE

▷··· STARTING POINT	···✗ DESTINATION
VIEJAS MOUNTAIN TRAILHEAD	**VIEJAS MOUNTAIN**
🍺 BREWERY	HIKE TYPE
MCILHENNEY BREWING COMPANY	**STRENUOUS**
🐾 DOG FRIENDLY	📅 SEASON
YES	**OCTOBER—MAY**
$ FEES	🕐 DURATION
YES (ADVENTURE PASS)	**2 HOURS 40 MIN.**
🗺 MAP REFERENCE	↦ LENGTH
CLEVELAND NATIONAL FOREST	**3.2 MILES** (ROUND TRIP)
🔎 HIGHLIGHTS	〰 ELEVATION GAIN
PANORAMIC VIEWS, MOUNTAIN SUMMIT	**1,476 FEET**

MUNTZ RYE IPA

 HAZY GOLD

GRAPEFRUIT,
PINEAPPLE

PINEAPPLE,
WHITE WINE

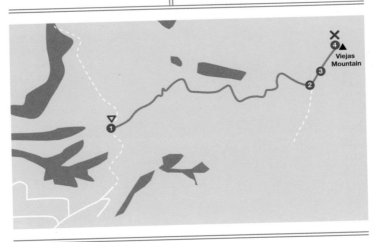

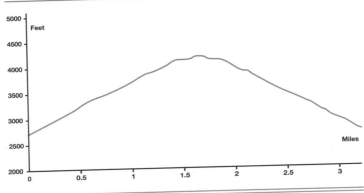

HIKE DESCRIPTION

Make your way up this deceptively demanding peak to 360-degree views of surrounding mountains and out to the Pacific Ocean. Top off the outing with an iconic New Zealand rye IPA from Mcilhenney Brewing Company.

Viejas Mountain is a sacred location where the Kumeyaay Indians mark the winter solstice. The name Viejas (Spanish for old women) is said to have originated with Spanish soldiers who intended to capture Kumeyaay Indians and force them to work at a mission. When the soldiers came to the valley, they only found the old women who had been unable to flee with the rest of the Kumeyaay.

This hike straddles the line between moderate and strenuous—it isn't too long and doesn't require any technical scrambling but does involve over a mile and a half of steep hiking with no shade. In hot, sunny conditions it can be a proper sufferfest that you don't want to underestimate: bring more water than you think you need and plenty of sun protection.

From the parking area, you'll head through an opening in the fence and follow the trail uphill towards the mountaintop. Most of the rocky, singletrack path heads up steeply through coastal sage scrub plants like California sagebrush, Cleveland sage, and manzanita. Small switchbacks weave through the landscape, which remains similar throughout the hike. If it becomes monotonous or disheartening to look up at how much you still have to climb, pause and look back at how far you've already come—you'll see your car get progressively smaller and the views over San Diego ever more expansive.

A little less than a mile and a half in, you'll reach a saddle and the ridgeline leading to the summit. From here, you can look east and see the Viejas Casino and Resort below you and the Cuyamaca Mountains in the distance. To the right of the trail, you'll see a cross-shaped rock alignment on the ground; this is used in the Kumeyaay Indians' solstice ceremony. The long axis points southeast to where the sun rises during the winter solstice. In the mid-1900s, vandals destroyed the cross, but it has since been recreated.

A diverging trail leads along the ridgeline to the right and reaches a small lookout in around 500 feet. Instead of taking it, you'll hike along the ridge to the left on a gradual incline and reach the summit, which is marked with two rock wall circles, a geological survey marker, and some tin cans with logbooks inside. From here, you'll return the way you came.

TURN-BY-TURN DIRECTIONS

1. From the pullout parking area off the dirt road, follow the unmarked trail going up the mountain on the right through a gap in the fence.
2. At 1.4 miles, reach a T-junction at the saddle on the ridge. On the right, you'll see a cross-shaped rock arrangement on the ground. Keep left at the T-junction, following the trail straight along the ridge.
3. At 1.5 miles, pass over a false summit with a metal pole; continue over boulders on the slightly overgrown trail towards the summit.
4. At 1.7 miles, reach the summit. Return the way you came.

FIND THE TRAILHEAD

From Mcilhenney Brewing Co. in central Alpine, head east on Alpine Blvd. After 0.7 miles, turn left onto E Victoria Dr. After 1.1 miles, turn right onto Anderson Rd. In 0.4 miles, the road transitions to National Forest land and becomes a gravel road. After another 0.4 miles, park at the dirt pullout on the left; the trailhead will be on the other side of the road.

MCILHENNEY BREWING COMPANY

Mcilhenney Brewing Co. opened in 2021, but owners Shawn and Jamie Mcilhenney have a multigenerational history with brewing in Alpine. Shawn, the head brewer, grew up brewing with his dad, Pat Mcilhenney, who opened Alpine Beer Company in 2002 in the same building Mcilhenney Brewing Co. occupies now. When Pat started Alpine Beer Co., there were fewer than 20 breweries in San Diego (now, there are over 150). Alpine Beer Co. merged with a larger brewing company and the Mcilhenneys stepped into different roles but retained their passion for brewing.

When Alpine Beer Co.'s original space became available, Shawn and Jamie jumped at the opportunity to begin again, and Mcilhenney Brewing Co. was born. Muntz is Shawn's improvement on one of Pat's most popular brews and uses hops from New Zealand. Pat was one of the first US brewers to use New Zealand hops, and this unfiltered brew, reminiscent of New Zealand white wine, is the brewery's most popular beer.

LAND MANAGER

Cleveland National Forest
10845 Rancho Bernardo Road, Suite 200
San Diego, CA 92127
(858) 673-6180
www.fs.usda.gov/cleveland
Map: data.fs.usda.gov/geodata/rastergateway/data3/32116/fstopo/
Viejas_Mountain_324511637_FSTopo.pdf

BREWERY/RESTAURANT

Mcilhenney Brewing Company
2363 Alpine Blvd.
Alpine, CA 91901
(619) 612-2207
www.mcilhenneybrewing.com/

Distance from trailhead: 2.6 miles

VOLCAN MOUNTAIN

A DELIGHTFUL WINDOW INTO SAN DIEGO'S MOUNTAINOUS BACKYARD

JULIAN

▷⋯ STARTING POINT	⋯✕ DESTINATION
VOLCAN MOUNTAIN TRAILHEAD	**VOLCAN MOUNTAIN**
🍺 BREWERY	▦ HIKE TYPE
JULIAN BEER COMPANY	**MODERATE**
🐾 DOG FRIENDLY	📅 SEASON
YES (LEASH REQUIRED)	**YEAR-ROUND**
$ FEES	🕐 DURATION
NONE	**2 HOURS 40 MIN.**
⌂ MAP REFERENCE	↦ LENGTH
POSTED AT TRAILHEAD	**5.4 MILES** (ROUND TRIP)
🔍 HIGHLIGHTS	〰 ELEVATION GAIN
SUMMIT VIEWS, WILDFLOWERS	**1,270 FEET**

6.3 %
ALCOHOL
CONTENT

ELEVATION 5353
COLD IPA

PALE GOLD

CITRUS,
FLORAL

CITRUS,
HOPPY

BITTERNESS

SWEETNESS

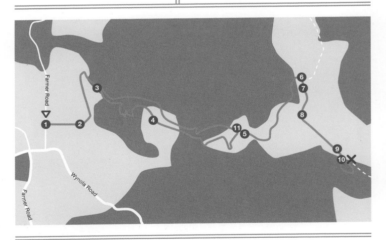

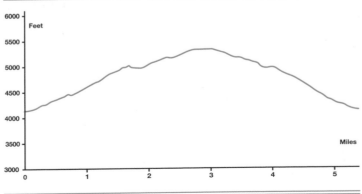

HIKE DESCRIPTION

Climb up to 5,353 feet and take in expansive views from the Salton Sea to the Pacific Ocean. Back in town, head to Julian Beer Co. and grab a brew that pays tribute to the elevation you just reached.

Volcan Mountain is one of Julian's prize hikes and the focal point of the 2,900-acre Volcan Mountain Wilderness Preserve. Moving through patchwork farmland, orchards, ranches, and preserve land, the trail you'll take features mixed conifer forests, oak woodland, wide open grassland, historic monuments, and far-reaching views.

From the parking area on Farmer Rd., you'll head down the gravel road between an apple orchard and a line of conifer trees until you reach the entrance to the Volcan Mountain Wilderness Preserve. Entering the preserve, you'll pass through a gateway sculpture made of hand-carved wooden beams and metal rods and designed by the internationally acclaimed artist and Julian local James Hubbell. The full entrance display came together thanks to local artisans and a dedicated group of volunteers who worked together every Sunday morning for over a year. Passing through the gateway, take a moment to admire the detail.

The dirt path gradually heads uphill through California buckwheat, sage, and oak trees. In the spring, this section also features a wide array of lush wildflowers including lupine, western wallflower, and purple owl's clover. If you notice animal scat along the trail, before you jump to blaming irresponsible dog owners, take a closer look—does it really look like dog poop? If the scat has fur, berries, or seeds, it could

be from a coyote, bobcat, or mountain lion. While you may see coyotes, you're unlikely to see either of the wild cats, which are typically nocturnal or crepuscular (active at dawn and dusk) and avoid humans. However, the scat is a sign that these elusive predators are in the area.

Just past the half-mile mark, you'll come to the turnoff for the Five Oaks Trail, a 1.2-mile "hikers only" detour that adds approximately 0.2 miles to the final route but is well worth its sweeping viewpoints and oak-tree canopies.

Once you rejoin the main Volcan Mountain Trail around 1.7 miles in, you'll pass through a shady section of oak and conifers before emerging on the grassy hillside leading to the summit. Further up the hillside, you'll pass an old stone chimney—remnants of an outpost used by astronomers who were considering Volcan mountain for the Hale Telescope. The famous telescope was eventually placed on Palomar Mountain instead.

At the peak, the trail circles the summit to showcase views from all directions. On your way down, when you reach the intersection of the Volcan Mountain Trail and the Five Oaks Trail, take the Volcan Mountain Trail to add some variety to your descent.

TURN-BY-TURN DIRECTIONS

1. From the street parking on Farmer Rd., head up the gravel road for the Volcan Mountain Wilderness Preserve.

2. At 0.1 miles, pass the entrance sign for the Volcan Mountain Wilderness Preserve. Continue straight on the gravel road for around 100 feet to the entrance gateway sculpture. Go in between the metal poles and continue on the Volcan Mountain Trail, passing a large interpretive map and a signpost listing the preserve's opening times.

3. At 0.6 miles, take the Five Oaks Trail on the right.

4. At 1.1 miles, pass a metal bench on the left looking out over Julian.

5. At 1.7 miles, meet back with the Volcan Mountain Summit Trail and turn right towards the summit.

6. At 2.3 miles, keep right on the Summit Trail, ignoring a private road on the left.

7. 100 feet further down the path, the stone remnants of the observatory outpost are on the right. There's a small trail spur leading close to the chimney, where you'll find an interpretive display. Return to the main trail.

8. At 2.5 miles, follow a trail spur on the right to an overlook with binoculars. Return to the main trail and continue straight.

9. At 2.8 miles, pass a small detour trail on the left leading to a viewpoint; skip this trail for now. Around 200 feet further down the trail, you'll pass the second connection with the viewpoint loop on the left (you'll take this on the way back) and reach the summit loop. Keep right to go around the loop, on which you'll see the Volcan Mountain Air Beacon, a picnic table, and an interpretive bulletin with information about birds of prey and rattlesnakes.

10. At 3.0 miles, close the summit loop. Take the viewpoint detour loop on the right that you skipped in the previous step. Once you rejoin the main trail, continue down the way you came, ignoring the trail spurs you took on the way up.

11. At 4.0 miles, come to the turn-off for the Five Oaks Trail. Instead of turning left, continue straight on the Volcan Mountain Summit Trail and follow it back to the trailhead.

FIND THE TRAILHEAD

From the Julian town hall and visitor center, head northwest on Main St., passing Julian Beer Co. After 0.1 miles, the road becomes Farmer Rd.; continue straight for 2.1 miles and then turn right onto Wynola Rd. 365 feet down Wynola road, turn left back onto Farmer Rd. After 0.1 miles, the sign for Volcan Mountain Wilderness Preserve and the trailhead will be on the right. Park on either side of Farmer Rd.

JULIAN BEER CO.

Julian Beer Co. was called Julian Brewing Company until head brewer Matt Pitman partnered up with the co-owner of Pizza Port, Vince Marsaglia, and his son Jeremy Marsaglia in 2016. The team completely remodeled the brewery, building all the tables, decking, and bar tops—an endeavor they hoped would take four months but in fact took two years. The new Julian Beer Co. officially opened its doors on July 4th, 2018.

The two-building brewery features twenty-one taps in each building, pizza and BBQ, and two acres of land behind the buildings that guests can wander while enjoying a pint. Pitman has been brewing for over ten years and his beers have won several awards, including a silver medal at the Brewers Cup of California for his Elevation 5353—named, of course, for the height of the mountain you just climbed.

LAND MANAGER

Volcan Mountain Wilderness Preserve
1209 Farmer Road at Wynola Rd.
Julian, CA 92036
(760) 765-4098
www.sdparks.org/content/sdparks/en/park-pages/VolcanMountain.html
Map: www.sdparks.org/content/dam/sdparks/en/pdf/Brochures
Miscellaneous/Volcan_Mountain_Brochure_FINAL.pdf

BREWERY/RESTAURANT

Julian Beer Co.
2307 Main St.
Julian, CA 92036
(760) 765-3757
www.julianbeerco.com/

Distance from trailhead: 2.3 miles

DEDICATION AND ACKNOWLEDGEMENTS

This book is first and foremost dedicated to the brewery owners, brewers, land managers, tribal organizations, and local hiking enthusiasts who shared their piece of the world with me, offered priceless recommendations, and welcomed both me and the book with open arms. *Beer Hiking Southern California* would not have happened without your passion for the outdoors and beer. Thank you.

When I had to abruptly change course from building a life in the English countryside in 2022, I didn't know what would come next. I owe many of the incredible work and travel opportunities that followed this upheaval to a client and mentor whom I feel lucky to consider a friend—Doug Mayer. Thank you for opening the door to a new world at a time when it would have been all too easy for me to spiral into self-pity.

Creating this book was more challenging, stressful, and time-consuming than I could ever have imagined. Dealing with a van leak during torrential rainstorms, hiking over 300 miles with an inflamed toe joint, and spending hundreds of hours holed up in a WeWork office, sometimes until 3 am, I was grateful for the unstinting support of the following people:

To my parents, Stuart Flashman and Jacqueline Richter, thank you for always believing in me, and for traveling to Southern California to do several of the hikes with me. Thank you for nurturing my sense of curiosity and teaching me an appreciation for plants and wildlife. You inspire me to work hard and try to make a difference in the world. To my sister, Sarah Flashman, thank you for your endless support, celebrating with me, eating grocery-store salads in a parking lot with me, and providing your indispensable insights on the world.

To my cousins Rick Flashman and Sabrina Batchelor, thank you for trusting me with your beautiful Sprinter van for six months and for offering your wisdom in the face of the many van-related challenges along the way.

To Colin Lauzon, who accompanied me on more of these hikes than anyone else: thank you for bringing snacks, taking photos, and encouraging me with wonderful puns every *step* of the way.

Thank you as well to all my good friends who have put up with constant book talk and listened to my voice notes from the trail for the past nine months. Thank you for enjoying good beer with me, being understanding when I've been less than communicative, and keeping me (relatively) sane. This list includes but is not limited to: Natalie Sheffield, Alice Beittel, Mateo Rudrich, Mark Luebrun, Blaire Burdey, Tyler Eddy, Chris Campbell, Ben Panico, Paul Boxing-Sarconi, Haley Thiltgen, Ernest Cheng, Aaron Ironworks-Hwang, Chris Lambert, and Angela Phan.

Sincere thanks to Richard Harvell and Ashley Curtis from Helvetiq. Thank you for taking a chance on me with this book. For listening to, trusting, and accommodating my requests and input on everything from cover design to brewery and hike choices. You've taken my rough drafts and guided them into a cohesive book. Thank you for your patience and advice when I thought I was drowning. I'm especially appreciative of Daniel Malak for his skill in creating the beautiful maps, profiles, and illustrations throughout the book. To everyone who's been a part of the Helvetiq team creating this book, thank you for allowing my writing, these breweries, and these hikes to shine.

A large appreciation to Casey Schreiner, author of *Day Hiking Los Angeles* and *Discovering Griffith Park*. Thank you for your generous advice and guidance on writing outdoor guidebooks to Southern California.

My gratitude also goes to the authors of the other books in the *Beer Hiking* series, including Carey Kish, Rachel Wood and Brandon Fralic, and Yitka Winn. Thank you for paving the way for these fantastic books. I'm honored to be a part of the series. Special thanks to Carey for permission to draw on his phrasing in parts of the Introduction.

To Renie Ritchie, Rik Mazzetti, and Jerri Mazzetti, thank you for your support and guidance in writing the land acknowledgement that appears in the Introduction.

A big thank you to Dayle Bingham, Barbara Tejada, and the other knowledgeable folks at the Chumash Indian Museum for helping me fact-check details in the Cave of Munits and Paradise Falls chapters.

Cheers and thank you to the many other wonderful people I've met along this journey and who've provided support and information as I developed *Beer Hiking Southern California*. Brewery managers, land managers, trail-maintenance teams, museums, tourism groups, brewers, brewery owners, wait staff, kitchen staff, marketing and communications staff, and so many others behind the scenes—thank you for making the Southern California beer hiking experience possible.

If I've forgotten anyone along the way, I apologize; thank you for your help.

--- FIRE ---
1 CUSTOM 5 FLIGHT
CHOCOLATE STOUT
DEL MARTIAN
AMBER
MEXICAN LAGER
PENITENT MAN
SAISON